A RETREAT WITH C. S. LEWIS

Other titles in the
A Retreat With... *Series:*

A Retreat With
C. S. Lewis

Yielding to a Pursuing God

Robert F. Morneau

ST. ANTHONY MESSENGER PRESS

Cincinnati, Ohio

Scripture citations are taken from the *New Revised Standard Version Bible*, copyright ©1989 by the Division of Christian Education of the National Council of Churches of Christ in the U.S.A. and used by permission.

Excerpts from the following works by C. S. Lewis are used by permission of the publishers: *C. S. Lewis: Poems*, edited by Walter Hooper, copyright ©1964, *The Four Loves*, copyright ©1960, *Letters of C. S. Lewis*, edited by W. H. Lewis, copyright ©1966, *Surprised by Joy*, copyright ©1955, all by Harcourt Brace Jovanovich, Publishers, New York; *The Lion, the Witch, and the Wardrobe*, copyright ©1970, *Mere Christianity*, copyright ©1952, *The Problem of Pain*, copyright ©1962, *The Silver Chair*, copyright ©1970, *The Voyage of the Dawn Treader*, copyright ©1954, all by Macmillan Publishers, New York; *A Grief Observed*, copyright ©1961, The Seabury Press, New York; *Till We Have Faces: A Myth Retold*, copyright ©1957, 1956 by C. S. Lewis PTE Ltd. and renewed 1985, 1984 by Arthur Owen Barfield, Harcourt, Inc.

Cover illustration by Steve Erspamer, S.M.
Cover and book design by Mary Alfieri
Electronic format and pagination by Sandy L. Digman

ISBN 0-86716-328-3

Published by St. Anthony Messenger Press
Printed in the U.S.A.

Contents

Introducing A Retreat With...

Twenty years ago I made a weekend retreat at a
Franciscan house on the coast of New Hampshire. The
retreat director's opening talk was as lively as a long-
range weather forecast. He told us how completely God
loves each one of us—without benefit of lively anecdotes
or fresh insights.

As the friar rambled on, my inner critic kept up a
sotto voce commentary: "I've heard all this before." "Wish
he'd say something new that I could chew on." "That
poor man really doesn't have much to say." Ever hungry
for manna yet untasted, I devalued any experience of
hearing the same old thing.

After a good night's sleep, I awoke feeling as peaceful
as a traveler who has at last arrived safely home. I walked
across the room toward the closet. On the way I passed
the sink with its small framed mirror on the wall above.
Something caught my eye like an unexpected presence. I
turned, saw the reflection in the mirror and said aloud,
"No wonder he loves me!"

This involuntary affirmation stunned me. What or
whom had I seen in the mirror? When I looked again, it
was "just me," an ordinary person with a lower-than-
average reservoir of self-esteem. But I knew that in the
initial vision I had seen God-in-me breaking through like
a sudden sunrise.

At that moment I knew what it meant to be made in
the divine image. I understood right down to my size
eleven feet what it meant to be loved exactly as I was.

Only later did I connect this revelation with one granted to the Trappist monk-writer Thomas Merton. As he reports in *Conjectures of a Guilty Bystander*, while standing all unsuspecting on a street corner one day, he was overwhelmed by the "joy of being...a member of a race in which God Himself became incarnate.... There is no way of telling people that they are all walking around shining like the sun."

As an absentminded homemaker may leave a wedding ring on the kitchen windowsill, so I have often mislaid this precious conviction. But I have never forgotten that particular retreat. It persuaded me that the Spirit rushes in where it will. Not even a boring director or a judgmental retreatant can withstand the "violent wind" that "fills the entire house" where we dwell in expectation (see Acts 2:2).

So why deny ourselves any opportunity to come aside awhile and rest on holy ground? Why not withdraw from the daily web that keeps us muddled and wound? Wordsworth's complaint is ours as well: "The world is too much with us." There is no flu shot to protect us from infection by the skepticism of the media, the greed of commerce, the alienating influence of technology. We need retreats as the deer needs the running stream.

An Invitation

This book and its companions in the *A Retreat With...* series from St. Anthony Messenger Press are designed to meet that need. They are an invitation to choose as director some of the most powerful, appealing and wise mentors our faith tradition has to offer.

Our directors come from many countries, historical eras and schools of spirituality. At times they are teamed to sing in close harmony (for example, Francis de Sales, Jane de Chantal and Aelred of Rievaulx on spiritual friendship). Others are paired to kindle an illuminating fire from the friction of their differing views (such as Augustine of Hippo and Mary Magdalene on human sexuality). All have been chosen because, in their humanness and their holiness, they can help us grow in self-knowledge, discernment of God's will and maturity in the Spirit.

Inviting us into relationship with these saints and holy ones are inspired authors from today's world, women and men whose creative gifts open our windows to the Spirit's flow. As a motto for the authors of our series, we have borrowed the advice of Dom Frederick Dunne to the young Thomas Merton. Upon joining the Trappist monks, Merton wanted to sacrifice his writing activities lest they interfere with his contemplative vocation. Dom Frederick wisely advised, "Keep on writing books that make people love the spiritual life."

That is our motto. Our purpose is to foster (or strengthen) friendships between readers and retreat directors—friendships that feed the soul with wisdom, past and present. Like the scribe "trained for the kingdom of heaven," each author brings forth from his or her storeroom "what is new and what is old" (Matthew 13:52).

The Format

The pattern for each *A Retreat With...* remains the same; readers of one will be in familiar territory when they move on to the next. Each book is organized as a seven-session retreat that readers may adapt to their own schedules or to the needs of a group.

Day One begins with an anecdotal introduction called "Getting to Know Our Directors." Readers are given a telling glimpse of the guides with whom they will be sharing the retreat experience. A second section, "Placing Our Directors in Context," will enable retreatants to see the guides in their own historical, geographical, cultural and spiritual settings.

Having made the human link between seeker and guide, the authors go on to "Introducing Our Retreat Theme." This section clarifies how the guide(s) are especially suited to explore the theme and how the retreatant's spirituality can be nourished by it.

After an original "Opening Prayer" to breathe life into the day's reflection, the author, speaking with and through the mentor(s), will begin to spin out the theme. While focusing on the guide(s)' own words and experience, the author may also draw on Scripture, tradition, literature, art, music, psychology or contemporary events to illuminate the path.

Each day's session is followed by reflection questions designed to challenge, affirm and guide the reader in integrating the theme into daily life. A "Closing Prayer" brings the session full circle and provides a spark of inspiration for the reader to harbor until the next session.

Days Two through Six begin with "Coming Together in the Spirit" and follow a format similar to Day One. Day Seven weaves the entire retreat together, encourages a continuation of the mentoring relationship and concludes with "Deepening Your Acquaintance," an envoi to live the theme by God's grace, the director(s)' guidance and the retreatant's discernment. A closing section of Resources serves as a larder from which readers may draw enriching books, videos, cassettes and films.

We hope readers will experience at least one of those memorable "No wonder God loves me!" moments. And we hope that they will have "talked back" to the mentors, as good friends are wont to do.

A case in point: There was once a famous preacher who always drew a capacity crowd to the cathedral. Whenever he spoke, an eccentric old woman sat in the front pew directly beneath the pulpit. She took every opportunity to mumble complaints and contradictions— just loud enough for the preacher to catch the drift that he was not as wonderful as he was reputed to be. Others seated down front glowered at the woman and tried to shush her. But she went right on needling the preacher to her heart's content.

When the old woman died, the congregation was astounded at the depth and sincerity of the preacher's grief. Asked why he was so bereft, he responded, "Now who will help me to grow?"

All of our mentors in *A Retreat With...* are worthy guides. Yet none would seek retreatants who simply said, "Where you lead, I will follow. You're the expert." In truth, our directors provide only half the retreat's content. Readers themselves will generate the other half.

As general editor for the retreat series, I pray that readers will, by their questions, comments, doubts and decision-making, fertilize the seeds our mentors have planted.

And may the Spirit of God rush in to give the growth.

Gloria Hutchinson
Series Editor
Conversion of Saint Paul, 1995

Getting to Know Our Director

Introducing C. S. Lewis

Clives Staples Lewis, one of the most significant
Christian apologists of the twentieth century, was born in
Belfast, Northern Ireland, on November 29, 1898. He died
at his home in Oxford, England, sixty-four years later on
November 22, 1963, the same day that President John F.
Kennedy was assassinated. Because of this international
tragedy, Lewis's death went unnoticed by many.

Consider the years 1898-1963: dates on a tombstone.
The span of years, the length of a life, is important, but
what is more meaningful is the dash between the dates.
What happened in the sixty-four years of that one life?
More than we might have imagined. Lewis used his gifts
as a scholar, teacher, storyteller, apologist and friend in
powerful ways. He lived his life to the full. Such a person
serves well as a retreat director.

Lewis's father, Albert (1863-1929), was a Belfast
Corporation County solicitor. In reflecting on his father's
life, C. S. Lewis noted a major limitation: his father's
incapacity for happiness. But one of his father's great gifts
to his two sons was a passion for old books. Beginning
early in life we see C. S. Lewis as a bibliophile, a lover of
books.

When Lewis was just nine, his mother, Flora
Hamilton (1862-1908), died of cancer. This tragedy deeply
affected the whole family. In fact, her husband never got
over the loss. Her other son, nicknamed "Warnie," was

also deeply scarred by her untimely death. Flora
Hamilton Lewis had attended Queen's University in
Belfast and gained honors in logic and mathematics. Her
literary son's romantic side did not come from her
intellectual temperament.

In his autobiographical work, *Surprised by Joy*, Lewis
discusses his relationship with his parents and brother;
his movement from atheism to Christianity; the various
influences, positive and negative, that shaped his interior
life; and his experiences of joy—those moments of
mysterious longing for beauty, truth, love and goodness.
Although his conversion to Christianity was made
"official" at age thirty-three, the process of becoming a
disciple of Jesus was gradual and evolutionary. God kept
surprising this brilliant, intense scholar with feelings of
enigmatic joy.

The autobiography also tells of Lewis's early years of
education. After his mother's death he was sent to
Hertfordshire in England. It was a huge mistake. This
school, as well as two others—Campbell College and
Malvern College—proved unsatisfactory to the needs and
sensitivities of the young Lewis. He was temperamentally
unfit for the rough environment and impersonalism of
these institutions. Eventually his intellectual formation
fell into the hands of an Irishman, W. T. Kirkpatrick. His
guidance proved to be just what was needed: personal
attention, strong rationality, appreciation for and
development of the gifts of the imagination. It was with
this new mentor that Lewis discovered and devoured the
writings of George MacDonald. (MacDonald was a
Scottish novelist, poet and former minister who also
wrote children's stories and allegorical fantasies for
adults.)

C. S. Lewis, whose friends called him "Jack," turned
nineteen in 1917. Along with his brother Warnie, he

participated in World War I. Jack was sent with the British troops to France. Within the year he was wounded and eventually discharged. The experience radically affected his life. One specific event is worthy of note. A fellow soldier, "Paddy" Moore, and Lewis made an agreement. If either of them would be killed, the survivor would tend to the other's surviving parent. Paddy Moore was killed and Jack, faithful to the promise made, cared for Paddy's mother, Janie Moore, until her death in 1951, a responsibility that was demanding and at times frustrating. C. S. Lewis was a promise-maker and a promise-keeper. This event reveals the quality of his integrity.

After the war Lewis entered Oxford University and in 1923 received a Triple First. He stayed on at Oxford for thirty-one years, lecturing, tutoring and writing. During the Second World War, Lewis was on the BBC and assisted in civil defense as a private citizen. In 1954 he was invited to teach Medieval and Renaissance Literature at Cambridge. This was his last teaching post.

Placing Our Director in Context

C. S. Lewis's life was dominated by a male environment: male schools, war experiences, the university setting. Women were insignificant in his social life. In 1952 he met a poet/novelist with whom he had been corresponding for some time. Her name was Helen Joy Davidman. She had two sons and eventually divorced her abusive American husband. When legal problems arose regarding Joy's remaining in England, Lewis married her—perhaps more out of an act of kindness than of passionate love. She developed cancer in 1957 but lived until 1960. During those years their love for each other deepened, opening for Lewis a whole new life of affectivity. Her death and his mourning were recorded in his diary, *A Grief Observed*. These events are also effectively portrayed in the two film versions of *Shadowlands*.

Lewis would live another three years, struggling to overcome his loss, struggling to deal with his brother Warnie's alcoholism, struggling to deepen his faith in a mysterious God of so many surprises. Out of that struggle Jack Lewis's creativity took on a new depth. And we are the beneficiaries of his joyful surprises and observations of grief.

DAY ONE

The Great Surprise
Joy

Introducing Our Retreat Theme

As I read through the writings of C. S. Lewis I see his life as one in which an unrelenting God is in pursuit of a gifted creature. The question is not whether God has sufficient speed to catch the fleeing soul, but whether this individual, Clives Staples Lewis, would surrender his will to divine purposes. Lewis did say yes to God and in this retreat we will focus on how that happened.

A brief overview of our seven-day journey together is in order. This first day our theme is joy, an elusive but profound experience that transformed the soul of C. S. Lewis. Taking a phrase from Wordsworth, "surprised by joy," Lewis describes the experience as one which is both ecstactic and painful, comforting and challenging. Joy is that sudden longing and desire for the fullness of truth, goodness and beauty. Joy is another name for a God of light, love and life.

In a culture of melancholy and loneliness, we need a mentor who not merely speaks about joy but who lived this grace as well. Using his book *Surprised by Joy* as a resource, we can pray over the deepest desires and longings of the human spirit. It may even be a prayer time that leads to laughter.

Joy is linked intimately with love. In fact, joy and

peace are love's byproducts. C. S. Lewis studies the
meaning of love, experiencing this virtue in his innermost
being. He knew himself to be loved by Joy Davidman, by
his close friends, by God. His work *The Four Loves*
provides material for meditation and a framework for
evaluating the loves in our own lives. This will be the
content of our prayer for Day Two.

Day Three provides an opportunity to pray over
those obstacles that block us from experiencing a
pursuing God. The theme for this day is conversion,
which Dorothy Day describes as "a falling in love with
God that frees us to reach out to those who are in pain."
Lewis was a realist. He was not afraid to call sin by name
and to challenge himself and others to turn from
selfishness to altruistic love. In his instructive work *Mere
Christianity* there is much to enlighten us regarding the
nature and process of conversion.

If we are being asked to say yes to God, to yield to
the divine purpose, to surrender our very selves to the
Lord, we want to ground that decision in truth. This will
be the theme for Day Four. C. S. Lewis could experience
the joy of beauty because he hungered for the peace of
truth. A resource for this day will be the *Chronicles of
Narnia*, a seven-volume series that tells in narrative form
how four young people journey into the land of truth.
Our time journeying with them is well spent.

In every retreat we seek to understand not only God's
identity, but our own as well. Who are we? Or perhaps
more exactly, *whose* are we? All of us struggle with false
identification, with illusions, with issues of control,
autonomy, narcissism. To strip away the false self and
come naked before the Lord just as we are is a major step
in our spiritual travels. The question of identity emerges
consistently in the writing of Lewis, but there is one
particular work, *Till We Have Faces*, that addresses this

issue by means of allegory. One of the goals of this retreat will be to have a clearer view of our face and a firmer understanding of our own voice. C. S. Lewis will guide us in seeking an answer to the question: Whose am I?

There are tragedies and sorrows in every life. The enigma of suffering and evil plagues the human heart. These mysteries cry out for an answer or at least an explanation that confronts their apparent absurdity. Lewis's *The Problem of Pain*, though ultimately unsatisfactory, offers material for serious prayer. No one can adequately explain pain and suffering. Perhaps in prayer, however, we will be given the grace to embrace this dimension of life and not let it be destructive of our faith life.

The seventh and final day of our retreat will have as its theme the reality of death and the possibility of resurrection. C. S. Lewis experienced the death of his mother—an overwhelming loss for the young boy. Then, falling in love late in life, Lewis lost his wife Joy Davidman to cancer. Lewis, as a thinker and writer, felt compelled to "make sense" of these experiences. His reflections here are extremely personal and moving. As fellow pilgrims we can participate in his experience and perhaps come to a new understanding of the role that death plays in our life.

A third-grade teacher from Grand Rapids, Michigan, told me this past year that in her twenty-six years of teaching, last year's class was by far the most difficult. But, she said: "After lunch I would read passages from C. S. Lewis's *Chronicles of Narnia* and every single student paid attention and asked for more. Something in those stories gave the children a certain level of peace."

If Lewis can touch the hearts of children, he surely can touch the hearts of us adults. The overall theme for these days is God's unceasing pursuit of his people—us.

Our challenge is to yield to this mystery of Love and unite our will with God's divine plan, the salvation of the world.

Under this umbrella of God's pursuit and our yielding we will hear C. S. Lewis speak of the joy resulting from God's surprising graces, the call to love and friendship, the need for conversion at the deepest recesses of our being, the importance of truth, our search for identity, the problem of suffering and the mystery of death. In these next seven days, or whatever time frame you use, the invitation is to a prayerful reflection on these themes. Perhaps we, too, like Lewis, will be surprised by joy.

C. S. Lewis experienced a kind of joy that was different from the popular meaning of the word. It was not a joy based on a particular good known and possessed. For Lewis, joy was "an unsatisfied desire which is itself more desirable than any other satisfaction."[1] At the heart of joy was an inconsolable longing for beauty, goodness and truth. As Lewis moved from the darkness of atheism into the light of Christianity he would come to realize that joy was a deep hunger and thirst for God.

Lewis first encountered joy by gazing at distant hills and reading the sagas contained in mythology. Nature and story triggered something deep in his soul that yearned and pined for more, more beauty, more truth, more presence. The created world, for all its splendor and glory, was simply not sufficient to satisfy the deepest longings and desires of the soul. Not even friendship and human love, beautiful and holy as they are, could offer complete fulfillment. Joy ultimately was an experience of heaven and, as it was for Moses, who was unable to enter the promised land, it would be only through the gate of death that this complete joy would be experienced.

As our retreat director, C. S. Lewis raises the question of the meaning of joy on our journey, both as individuals and as members of larger communities (family, nation, world). Where do we find our joy? Are all human joys partial and, if so, why? Is our concept of God one that includes joy or is that conception of the Deity more cognitive and ethical than it is affective and fascinating? In today's session, we will hear Lewis speaking to us from the page of his autobiography *Surprised by Joy: The Shape of My Early Life.*

Opening Prayer

Gracious and loving God, your goodness and fidelity fill the earth, giving us cause for great joy. May your Spirit empower us to see your beauty and discern your will. May that same Spirit make us joyful instruments of your love in our fragile and broken world. We ask this through Christ our Lord.

RETREAT SESSION ONE

It is in the context of his mother's death that C. S. Lewis gives us our first point for meditation. Lewis had prayed that his mother might live, expecting that God would answer his request made in faith. Lewis's mother died. Reflecting on this experience at the time of his conversion at age thirty-three, Lewis confesses that his beliefs in early youth were essentially irreligious. Here is a passage from that confession:

I had approached God, or my idea of God, without

> love, without awe, even without fear. He was, in my
> mental picture of this miracle, to appear neither as
> Savior nor as Judge, but merely as a magician; and
> when He had done what was required of Him I
> supposed He would simply—well, go away.[2]

Joy is grounded in the truth of things, its foundation is in
reality. But the encounter with truth, the truth of
ourselves or God or the world, is conditioned by our
disposition. We cannot apprehend God unless love, awe
and even fear reside in our hearts. God simply will not be
manipulated; God will not be turned into a magician.

Consider: *When you come to prayer, what are the dispositions
in your heart? What are the attitudes you bring to this sacred
encounter with the divine presence?*

A core question of every retreat is our image of God. Who
is this God whom we approach, or more accurately, who is
this God who continuously approaches us? In the epistles
of Saint John we are told time and again that "God is
love." And is not love the ultimate source of joy (and
peace)? C. S. Lewis's inconsolable longing was for love,
that union and intimacy with God which alone can satisfy
the soul's deepest thirst.

Consider: *Is your idea of God that of a loving Creator,
Redeemer, Sanctifier?*

Our mentor speaks about God in terms of being savior
and judge. Behind these concepts are the mysteries of
lostness and sin. God is a healing, saving Lord; God is one
who holds us accountable, responsible for the words and
deeds that shape our history and touch the lives of others.
Lewis rejects romanticism and perceives God as
compassionate (savior) and demanding (judge). Our
generation needs to retrieve a theology that is honest in

dealing with the dark side of life. If joy is connected with the truth of things, then only by living in the presence of a real God can we come to know the grace and gift of joy.

Consider: *How does God "save" you? Where in your life do you feel God's judgment?*

Our second point for meditation looks at joy and the presence of good people. Joy is mediated through people who live lives of love and concern. For Lewis joy was not only felt in nature or mythology or deep silence, it was also experienced in human relationships. A keen observer, Lewis notes certain qualities in his uncle's wife that deeply touched him: kindness, good sense, hospitality, acceptance. Though not the ultimate joy that we desire, here are partial joys that are clues and hints of something greater to come. Lewis appreciated both the minor and major joys of life.

> During these talks our attention was fixed not on one another but on the subject. His [Uncle Joe's] Canadian wife I have already mentioned. In her also I found what I like best—an unfailing, kindly welcome without a hint of sentimentality, unruffled good sense, the unobtrusive talent for making all things at all times as cheerful and comfortable as circumstances allowed. What one could not have one did without and made the best of it.[3]

Way back in the Book of Genesis we hear tell that it is not good for man (or woman) to be alone. We have this deep need to belong, to be connected on life's journey. Such is the human condition. We are social by nature. We long for that kind, warm welcome that we call hospitality. The sense of isolation and loneliness is strong in our culture. People feel excluded and marginalized. It's no surprise that there is such joylessness, such sadness. The ministry of hospitality is a direct conduit for joy. Lewis's aunt imaged God by welcoming her nephew with unfailing kindness.

Consider: *What is your level of hospitality toward friends, strangers and God? In what ways do you give them the opportunity to experience joy?*

William Wordsworth gives us some unruffled good sense in this verse: "'It is an injury' said I, 'to this day / To think of any thing but present joy.'" It does take some years of living to develop the art of living in the present moment. Joy is almost impossible without it since we will always be pulling ourselves out of the now to review the past or anticipate the future, thereby missing the moment. Joy demands the good sense of presence, being where you are with both feet firmly planted. There will be a cost here. We will also have to embrace griefs as fully as joys. But is there any other way truly to live?

C. S. Lewis would not allow us to identify joy with lesser realities, such as cheerfulness and making things comfortable. Yet people who sensitively make life pleasant for others are cultivating a land that makes joy welcome. Indeed, many of the joys of life are missed because of mean-spiritedness and the squalor of life. It is a bonus when a person who makes life comfortable and cheerful does this in an unobtrusive manner. Lewis appreciated such talent and would not let it pass by without gratitude.

Consider: *Do you have the talent to make life cheerful for others, thereby disposing them to experience the deep joys of life? How will you invest this talent?*

In our third point for meditation, we focus on the connection between joy and comprehending the essence of things as they are. Again we see Lewis as a people

watcher. This time he notes a talent of one of his teachers,
Jenkin, who astounded Lewis by his ability to enjoy
everything. Most of us are quite selective in life,
separating out whatever is ugly, unpleasant or simply
distasteful. Not Lewis's teacher. His attitude was one
of total immersion in life, be the waters therein icy,
lukewarm or scalding. Jenkin's attitude was for a full
baptism.

> But Jenkin seemed to be able to enjoy everything;
> even ugliness. I learned from him that we should
> attempt a total surrender to whatever atmosphere
> was offering itself at the moment; in a squalid town
> to seek out those very places where its squalor rose
> to grimness and almost grandeur, on a dismal day to
> find the most dismal and dripping wood, on a
> windy day to seek the windiest ridge. There was no
> Betjemannic irony about it; only a serious, yet
> gleeful, determination to rub one's nose in the very
> quiddity of each thing, to rejoice in its being (so
> magnificently) what it was.[4]

One of the most influential spiritual writers of the
eighteenth century was Jean-Pierre de Caussade (1675-
1751). His classic text *The Sacrament of the Present Moment*
presents a spirituality of "quiddity," of rubbing your nose
in the essence of things. Father de Caussade writes:
"Everything turns to bread to nourish me, soap to wash
me, fire to purify me, and a chisel to fashion me in the
image of God."[5] Nothing, save sin, is excluded as an
instrument of God's providential care. We have here a
principle upon which one could build a rule of life.

Consider: *How does God nourish, wash, purify and chisel
you?*

Surrendering to things as they are was not an easy
experience for C. S. Lewis. He identifies himself as the

prodigal son who came home screaming and kicking. It took many years for Lewis to reach that mature level of spirituality in which surrender comes as naturally as breathing. Always there is our human will, with its own plans and designs, that seeks control. No surprise then that much of life passes us by. Obedience to the current atmosphere creates the possibility of joy. Resistance to the way life is assures us of a life of anxiety and fear.

Was George Herbert correct when he wrote: "...All worldly joys go less / To the one joy of doing kindnesses"? Jenkin taught Lewis "to rub his nose in the quiddity of things." Certainly this is one approach to joy, one that I would personally affirm. And part of the quiddity of things is human need, the need for shelter, clothing, food, employment. I have witnessed great joy as people came along with a helping hand and a compassionate heart and rubbed their noses in the needs of others. No one can describe the radiance of joy that stems from the doing of kindness. Again we have come full circle: joy results from love and love finds expression in kindness.

For Reflection

It is a blessing to be surprised by joy, whether in nature, in mythology, in friendship, in encounters with grace. Lewis would often speak of this longing, yearning delight that he calls joy:

> And Lucy felt running through her that deep shiver of gladness which you only get if you are being solemn and still.[6]

> We have known great joys together.[7]

> Joy silenced me.[8]

Joy is central to the spiritual journey. It is the telltale sign
of love, of God's presence within the individual and the
community. It is one of the fruits of the Holy Spirit that
fills our lives with radiance and enthusiasm. Joy does
silence us but also makes us shout with jubilation.

- *How might God be calling you to enter more deeply into
  the given opportunities for joy?*

- *What great joys have you shared with loved ones? In what
  ways do you express your gratitude?*

Closing Prayer

*"...All worldly joys go less
To the one joy of doing kindnesses."*
　　　　　　　　　—George Herbert

Lord, it is only by yielding to your pursuing presence,
that we come to know the joy of your peace.
Give us the gift of wonder to be surprised at your
　　　many comings:
in affection, in butterflies, in the midnight moon.
Help us then to give that joy away
to those who find life burdensome.

Notes

1 C. S. Lewis, *Surprised by Joy: The Shape of My Early Life* (New York:
Harcourt Brace Jovanovich, Publishers, 1955), pp. 17-18.

2 *Surprised by Joy*, p. 21.

3 *Surprised by Joy*, p. 43.

4 *Surprised by Joy*, p. 199.

5 Jean-Pierre de Caussade, *The Sacrament of the Present Moment*, trans.

by Kitty Muggeridge (San Francisco: Harper & Row, 1966), pp. 71-72.

[6] C. S. Lewis, *The Voyage of the Dawn Treader* (New York: The Macmillan Company, 1954), p. 240.

[7] C. S. Lewis, *The Last Battle* (New York: The Macmillan Company, 1956), p. 99.

[8] C. S. Lewis, *Till We Have Faces* (Grand Rapids, Mich.: William B. Eerdmans Publishing Company, 1956), p. 306.

DAY TWO

Four of a Kind?
Love

Coming Together in the Spirit

In 1960, three years before his death, Lewis wrote *The Four Loves,* an analysis of the various ways in which we humans transcend ourselves and are united to the world, others and God. This book was written during Lewis's marriage to Joy Davidman, a marriage of short duration because of her untimely death, but a marriage in which Lewis experienced love in profound ways. Much of the material in *The Four Loves* flows from first-hand experience.

Lewis's anatomy of love falls into four categories.

1) Affection (*storge*) is the first form. It is a certain fondness for others and is the most instinctive kind of love, often accompanied by a fierce jealousy. Lewis asserts that "affection is responsible for nine-tenths of whatever solid and durable happiness there is in our natural lives."[1] Affection is more than feeling and must be filled with common sense lest it turn sour through excessive sentimentality.

2) Friendship (*philia*) is a form of love in which partners are side by side, not face to face, bonded through a common interest. Lewis considers friendship a necessary love for full human maturity and happiness. He raises a question in one of his letters: "Is any pleasure on earth as great as a circle of Christian friends by a fire?"

Friendship implies equality, mutual responsibility, often seeing and sharing the same truth. It is one of life's greatest graces.

3) Sexual love (*eros*) is a third form of love. It is physical but much more than that. It is a longing for the beloved that takes the lover outside of himself or herself. There is a deep mystery about this love which defies understanding. Once eros enters the soul everything changes. Sometimes identified as romantic love, this passion has a built-in ambiguity—it can be highly creative and life-giving, or it can be thoroughly destructive, even smelling of death.

4) Charity (*agape*), for Lewis, is a gift-love, whereas the first three forms of love are all human loves, that is, need-loves. Charity is divine love, a response of love to a God who first loves us. Each of the four loves is good in its proper place, but the most powerful and most important is agape. This is God's love for us and our willed response of love for God. Divine charity is a giving, not a getting love.

Defining Our Thematic Context

If C. S. Lewis was surprised by joy, he was fascinated by the mystery of love. On this second day of retreat we gaze intently at the reality of love, its different forms, its power to change us, its centrality in our Christian lives.

Opening Prayer

God of extravagant love, teach us your love to know and do, and, if it is your will, to feel. Free us from our self-centeredness and apathy. Fire us with the holy flame of your Spirit that we might give ourselves without reserve to your divine plan of reconciliation. May Jesus dwell always in our hearts, empowering us to make present to your world your eternal concern. Teach us, Lord, please teach us to love and to know intimately that we are loved by you.

RETREAT SESSION TWO

Today's first point for meditation recognizes that love is a risky business. In Thomas Hardy's classic *The Return of the Native*, the author uses an image of an autumn-hatched bird, which, because of the impending winter, has little chance of surviving, to depict a person who once loved, was rejected, and now attempts to love again. Will that second love, surrounded by scars and hurt, be able to survive? Hardy calls our attention to the fact that love is vulnerable, fragile and in need of protection and support. C. S. Lewis articulates well this dimension of love:

> To love at all is to be vulnerable. Love anything, and your heart will certainly be wrung and possibly be broken. If you want to make sure of keeping it intact, you must give your heart to no one, not even to an animal. Wrap it carefully round with hobbies and little luxuries; avoid all entanglements; lock it up safe in the casket or coffin of your selfishness. But in that casket—safe, dark, motionless, airless—it will change. It will not be broken; it will become unbreakable, impenetrable, irredeemable. The alternative to tragedy, or at least to the risk of tragedy, is damnation. The only place outside Heaven where you can be perfectly safe from all the dangers and perturbations of love is Hell.[2]

Love is a risky business. No surprise that we are well practiced in protecting ourselves with reticence, distancing geography, a noncommittal life-style. If you say nothing there can be no criticism; if you set yourself apart, you are beyond harm's arrow; if you refuse to make decisions or assume responsibility, failures cannot be attributed to your ledger. Love makes us vulnerable, such is its nature. Love also affords us the opportunity of union and intimacy with God and others, a union we know as happiness (even heaven).

Consider: *Why does the expectation of immunity from love's hurt persist among us?*

Idolatry was clearly a sin in the Old Testament. Moses came upon his people worshipping a golden calf. Seldom do people confess the sin of idolatry in our times, yet we need but glance around us to see many idols. Money, power, prestige, possessions, technology can easily move in and claim the heart's time and energy. Lewis mentions "hobbies and little luxuries" as things that remove us from the land of love and plant us in the world of things. We substitute some lesser good for relationships and wonder why we are not happy.

Consider: *Are the hobbies and luxuries in your life kept in their proper place?*

C. S. Lewis is a realist. If you love, you may well face tragedy. The parent who receives that dreaded 3 A.M. phone call from the police reporting a teenager's death experiences tragedy because the parent's love is so deep. Without love the news does not devastate the heart. What Lewis is saying is that love simply is not safe, safe in the sense that if you possess this love, you will be immune from life's anguish and pain. If this is difficult, the alternative is worse. Not to love is damnation. It is the confining of self into a coffin of selfishness and utter darkness.

Consider: *What is the correlation in your life between love and tragedy?*

Our second meditation point considers "Love: Gift or Need?" In Shakespeare's Sonnet 116, the bard proclaims: "Love is not love / Which alters when it alteration finds...." In his two long-term relationships with women (Mrs. Janie "Minto" Moore, the older woman he called "my mother," and Joy Davidman—later Joy Gresham Lewis), Lewis remained faithful, compassionate and attentive throughout their trying final illnesses. Nor was his love altered by the ways in which both women, to some extent, took advantage of his financial generosity. Would that our love were as constant as the poet suggests or as Lewis exhibited for Minto and Joy. From experience we know that sometimes our love does alter us, as when a son or daughter fails to send that thank-you note or a friend fails to sustain the relationship or the unkind word is spoken. We cross people off our list because our love is based on need, not gift. C. S. Lewis is a defender of a higher love, one that is gratuitous because it is graced. He writes:

> Divine Love is Gift-love. The Father gives all He is and has to the Son. The Son gives Himself back to the Father, and gives Himself to the world, and for the world to the Father, and thus gives the world in Himself, back to the Father too. And what, on the other hand, can be less like anything we believe of God's life than Need-love? He lacks nothing, but our Need-love, as Plato saw, is "the son of Poverty." It is the accurate reflection in consciousness of our actual nature. We are born helpless. As soon as we are fully

conscious we discover loneliness. We need others
physically, emotionally, intellectually; we need them
if we are to know anything, even ourselves.[3]

In his poem "Matins," the priest-poet George Herbert's
concluding stanza reads:

Teach me your love to know
That this new light which now I see
May both the work and workman show
Then by a sunbeam I'll climb to thee.[4]

This powerful prayer petitions God for an experience of
the mystery of gift-love, a love that so transcends our
human capacity that it would cause despair were we not
empowered by the Holy Spirit. Agape, divine love, is
possible in our lives because the Spirit dwells within us.
True, our need-loves remain and will be major forces in
our daily living. But we are not limited to their demands.
Through Christ and his redemptive work, we now are
enabled to live lives of self-sacrifice and self-giving.

A good retreat question: With which person of the
Trinity—Father, Son, Spirit—do you have the strongest
relationship? Through Baptism we enter into the mystery
of grace and divine life. God's love here is one of self-
giving and so we encounter a God who is creator,
redeemer, sanctifier. As we mature in faith we are invited
into deeper and deeper union with our triune God. The
two central mysteries of Divine Love are the Incarnation
and the Trinity. We must pray for an experience and
understanding of these truths about gift-love.

Consider: *Which person of the Trinity speaks most deeply to
your heart? Why do you think this is so?*

In the first beatitude Jesus speaks about the poor in spirit
and how blessed they are. One thing is certain in life: we
are radically poor; we have an ultimate indigence. No

matter that we attempt to fill this poverty with degrees, bank accounts or large dwellings. The morning sun reminds us of our nakedness and need. Need-love, therefore, is legitimate and unavoidable. But, through grace, we are capable of expressing a love that emulates that of Jesus, a love so great as to lay down one's life for others. We are capable in the Spirit of gift-love.

In our third meditation point, we consider "Love and Friendship." One of the most powerful sections of the New Testament is Jesus' discourse in the Gospel of John, chapters 15-17. Jesus tells his disciples that they are no longer servants but friends, companions to whom he can reveal his innermost dreams and desires. Friendship is about sharing matters of the heart. It involves a profound, respectful intimacy that overflows into joy and fidelity. A retreat is a time of renewing friendship and seeking to grasp more clearly the mystery of this grace. C. S. Lewis treasured friendship as one of the great blessings in life. He writes:

> Friendship arises out of mere Companionship when two or more of the companions discover that they have in common some insight or interest or even taste which the others do not share and which, till that moment, each believed to be his own unique treasure (or burden). The typical expression of opening Friendship would be something like, "What? You too? I thought I was the only one." We can imagine that among those early hunters and warriors single individuals—one in a century? one in a thousand years?—saw what others did not; saw that the deer was beautiful as well as edible, that hunting was fun as well as necessary, dreamed that his gods might be not only powerful but holy. But as long as each of these percipient persons dies without finding a kindred soul, nothing (I suspect) will come of it; art or sport or spiritual religion will not be

born. It is when two such persons discover one
another, when, whether with immense difficulties
and semi-articulate fumbling or with what would
seem to us amazing and elliptical speed, they share
their vision—it is then that Friendship is born. And
instantly they stand together in an immense
solitude.[5]

Each person constructs his or her own world. It is
populated with certain values, a specific geography, a
tempo and disposition terribly unique, dreams and
memories that bear one's own fingerprints. This world
can be a lonely place if unshared. Such need not be the
case. Friendship means a sharing, partial to be sure, of
one's world with another. In it two or more people realize
that they have commonly held visions and values. Once
the risk of sharing takes place, never again will loneliness
be the central word in one's vocabulary.

Consider: *Make a list of your friends! What is the basis for
these loves?*

One of the cultural forces that impedes friendship is the
phenomenon of individualism and an exaggerated
emphasis on our autonomy. When freedom is stressed to
such a degree that it denies our interdependence, we are
in serious trouble. Some claim that the problem in
America today is loneliness. In other words, the problem
in our land is a lack of friendship and community. Retreat
calls us back to the miracle of dialogue—with God, with
others, with nature, with ourselves. One of the
outstanding biblical theologians of our day, Walter
Brueggemann, uses the expression: "serious conversation
leading to blessed communion." All friendship and
community is built upon that authentic and deep
conversation that leads to union. Through conversation
that is serious and deep we will be able to say: "What?

You too?" Indeed, we are not the only ones to desire justice and peace and love in our day.

Consider: *How many serious conversations have you had over the past month?*

The love that Lewis calls friendship cannot be planned or forced. To set out to make someone our friend is a deadly endeavor. However, we can and should create conditions in which friendships might arise. By taking time for prayer, by organizing a book club, by attending social events, we avail ourselves of opportunities in which serious conversation, a fundamental prerequisite of friendship, might occur. Passivity in this area is irresponsibility. We must be proactive in constructing a religious and social life in which friendship might be encountered.

For Reflection

Love, indeed, is a many splendored thing. Perhaps it doesn't come in as many varieties as ice cream but the flavors that are given are truly succulent. In the end, we will probably be asked only one question: "What was the quality of your love?" C. S. Lewis is a good guide in presenting us with the prism of love with its many facets. He offers us some concluding reflections:

> Every Christian would agree that a man's spiritual health is exactly proportional to his love for God.[6]

> To love and admire anything outside ourselves is to take one step away from utter spiritual ruin; though we shall not be well so long as we love and admire anything more than we love and admire God.[7]

Christian Love, either towards God or towards man,
is an affair of the will.[8]

- *What parish or other groups do you belong to that might
  lead to deep friendships?*

- *How will you make yourself "more available" to God in
  agape-love?*

Closing Prayer

"We come to God by love and not by navigation."

—Saint Augustine

God of extravagant love,
you who pursue us in great fidelity,
teach us again your love to know,
a love made visible in Jesus our Lord.
Send your Spirit of reverence and respect into our
    world so that the fires of your love might purge us
    of sin—our refusal to love—and fill us with your
    light and warmth.
Make us glad instruments of your love and mercy.
Amen. Alleluia.

Notes

[1] C. S. Lewis, *The Four Loves* (New York: Harcourt Brace Jovanovich,
    1960), p. 80.

[2] *The Four Loves*, p. 169.

[3] *The Four Loves*, pp. 11-12.

[4] George Herbert, "Matins," *George Herbert: The Country Parson, The
    Temple*, ed. with introduction by John N. Wall, Jr. (New York:
    Paulist Press, 1981).

[5] *The Four Loves*, pp. 96-97.

[6] *The Four Loves*, p. 13.

[7] C. S. Lewis, *Mere Christianity*, (New York: Macmillan, 1952), p. 113.

[8] *Mere Christianity*, p. 117.

DAY THREE

More than Mere Christianity
Conversion

Coming Together in the Spirit

Though Christians differ significantly on doctrinal
and moral issues, there is a high level of unanimity
regarding the need for conversion. Something has gone
wrong in history. Human freedom too often has turned
down the path of hatred, fear and sheer stupidity, dead
ending in extreme darkness. God calls us in Christ to
walk the way of peace, that is, the way of love, truth and
forgiveness. Every day we come to the intersections of sin
and grace; every day we venture more deeply into the
process of conversion.

C. S. Lewis experienced conversion, conversion to
theism in 1929, conversion to Christianity in 1931. Years
later he published his understanding of what it means to
be a Christian in *Broadcast Talks* (1942), *Christian Behavior*
(1943) and *Beyond Personality* (1944). In 1952 these three
works were put together in a single volume entitled *Mere
Christianity*.

Lewis knew from the inside the post-Christian
environment of England, for he himself had been there.
Understanding human psychology so well, Lewis began
the work of conversion by pre-evangelizing, by
presenting the reasonableness of the moral law and
human dignity. His lectures were preparing the ground

upon which God's seeds of grace might find a basic receptivity. He was successful. *Mere Christianity* paved the way and continues to pave the way for those who are called out of darkness into light.

Opening Prayer

> God of light and life,
> you call us out of the darkness of ignorance
> into the splendid truth of Christ.
> You call us from the death of sin
> into the Trinitarian life of Grace.
> Break our stubbornness with your gentle touch,
> cure our blindness in your extravagant mercy.
> Then, guided by the wisdom of your Spirit,
> we bring your justice and peace
> to our fragile and broken world.
> Grant this through Christ our Lord.

RETREAT SESSION THREE

Two of the most powerful stories in the New Testament are the narratives about the good Samaritan and the prodigal son. One deals with charity and the other with conversion. Both explore the manner in which God approaches us to bring salvation.

Lewis records his own experience of conversion, an experience of his prodigality but even more of God's extravagant mercy. Listen to the confession of a reluctant penitent:

In the Trinity Term of 1929 I gave in, and admitted

that God was God, and knelt and prayed; perhaps,
that night, the most dejected and reluctant convert
in England. I did not then see what is now the most
shining and obvious thing; the Divine humility
which will accept a convert even on such terms. The
Prodigal Son at least walked home on his own feet.
But who can duly adore that Love which will open
the high gates to a prodigal who is brought in
kicking, struggling, resentful, and darting eyes in
every direction for a chance of escape? The words
compelle intrare, compel them to come in, have been
so abused by wicked men that we shudder at them;
but, properly understood, they plumb the depth of
the Divine mercy. The hardness of God is kinder
than the softness of men, and His compulsion is our
liberation.[1]

The persistence of God is well delineated in Francis
Thompson's "The Hound of Heaven." God pursues us
"down the nights and down the days," and when grace
finally penetrates our rebellious hearts we give in, admit
God's faithful presence, kneel and pray. C. S. Lewis is
very clear: God takes the initiative and never gives up on
us. The invitation to conversion is a continual process and
a sign of God's deep desire to bring all people into the
paradise we call peace. And God works in a variety of
ways. Lewis comments in one of his letters that two
friends, Hugo Dyson and J. R. R. Tolkien, "were the
immediate human causes of my conversion."

Two years earlier, in 1929, Lewis had experienced a
"moment of illumination" on a bus when his resistance to
God began to melt. Then one September night in 1931 he
and Dyson, an Anglican, and Tolkien, a Catholic, talked
into the wee hours about how Lewis had failed to
approach the gospel with a "receptive imagination." His
friends enabled him to see that "the story of Christ is
simply a true myth: a myth working on us in the same

way as the others, but with this tremendous difference: That it *really happened*; and one must be content to accept it in the same way."[2]

Consider: *What are some of the human causes God uses to continue the conversion process in your life?*

Besides persistence God also has great patience in dealing with us human beings. Lewis uses the phrase "Divine humility" to express the way that God accepts back a begrudging sinner. Parents of certain teenagers who demonstrate defiance and hostility image God in their incredible humility and patience that refuse to give up, even in the face of rejection. Of course, the humility is complemented by a corresponding humor, as God and parents realize that all the resistance flows from a wealth of self-doubt and the struggle to discover one's own identity. Nonetheless, it is an amazing grace to experience acceptance by a God whom we find in our early days as unacceptable.

Consider: *What has been your experience of God's patience and humility? How do you image that patience in dealing with those who reject you?*

Isaiah the prophet reminds us that God's designs and plans are far different from our own. A priest I knew often said that "if you want to make God laugh, make plans!" God's plan is for our liberation; God wants us to be free and responsible. From our perspective it appears as if divine compulsion ("compel them to come in") infringes on our liberty, and that divine hardness negates God's gentleness. But the divine physician is not above using the knife if it will yield health and life. The process of conversion deals with the mystery of human freedom as it interfaces with the divine will. It should not be surprising that in this enigmatic field we struggle to understand how hardness and softness commingle, how compulsion and liberation are compatible.

Consider: *How has God brought about liberation in your life at the physical, psychological and spiritual levels?*

In our second meditation, we look at "Conversion: A Matter of Salvation." Christianity is serious business— indeed, a matter of life and death. The gospel contains imperatives which, when heeded, revolutionize our life and shape our destiny. C. S. Lewis felt the urgency of Christ's call, the vocation to become a new creature through the paschal mystery. Simply being nice on this human journey or developing one's potential, good as these are, do not assure salvation. Here is Lewis's perspective:

> We must not suppose that even if we succeeded in making everyone nice we should have saved their souls. A world of nice people, content in their own niceness, looking no further, turned away from God, would be just as desperately in need of salvation as a miserable world—and might even be more difficult to save. For mere improvement is no redemption, though redemption always improves people even here and now and will, in the end, improve them to a degree we cannot yet imagine. God became man to turn creatures into sons: not simply to produce better men of the old kind but to produce a new kind of man.[3]

Most of us have heard the playground counsel: "Be nice." If such were the case, the playground and the world could be very comfortable. Being nice includes things like small acts of courtesy: opening the door for the elderly, keeping silence in the movie theater, taking the dog out for a walk. Behavior to the contrary—insensitivity to the needs of others, human or animal—is reprehensible and indicates a need for a "minor" though not unimportant conversion. But salvation and true conversion, living lives centered on God and the divine will, transcends nicety by many light years. Here we are in the realm of charity and sacrifice, a giving of oneself even unto death. Discipleship is serious business. Being nice is only the prelude to the song of total love.

Consider: *Why is courtesy insufficient for discipleship?*

A claim is made today that many time-management books are the new spiritual manuals for our age. In deciding how to use effectively our limited time and energy, these works charge readers to draw up a mission statement and list their key values. Thousands of people have improved their work and found balance in their personal lives by these methods. I personally have found them most helpful. But again, is corporate or self-improvement enough to give one's life a radical reorientation? C. S. Lewis, I think, would affirm many of these improvement methods but would critique them in being too self-reliant when it comes to our faith life. Only grace can transform us at the level of our deepest being. We are not capable of self-salvation as we are of self-improvement.

Consider: *What techniques have you employed over the last five years to improve your life? Have these techniques affected the development of your faith life?*

Philosophers love to make distinctions. One example is the distinction between degree and kind. Joseph Smith is still Joseph Smith whether five, thirty-five or eighty-five. There will be different degrees of energy, insight and maturity throughout life's journey but the person is still a person. However, Joseph Smith is different in kind from the apple tree in his backyard. Though both the person and tree are creatures, not self-constructed, they are radically different kinds of creatures. So, too, regarding conversion. This spiritual process makes us into a new kind of person, one liberated from the old person entrapped in darkness and sin. As long as we live there will be an ongoing need for conversion, a matter of dying to the old self that Christ might live in us. Herein is salvation and the essence of conversion.

Consider: *How do you respond when the "old self" is reactivated? Can that response be improved?*

Now we look at conversion as a whole new life. Saint Paul experienced conversion in a dramatic fashion. The Risen Christ broke into Paul's life and at first he knew only blindness, confusion and fear. The initial shock of so much light and love (and guilt) left him traumatized. As Paul became accustomed to this whole new life he experienced the signs of sanctification, of authentic Christian conversion, that is, an increase of love, peace, joy. Lewis also experienced God's intervention and wrote about the meaning of sanctification, the meaning of this whole new life:

> Put right out of your head the idea that these are only fancy ways of saying that Christians are to read what Christ said and try to carry it out—as a man may read what Plato or Marx said and try to carry it out. They mean something much more than that. They mean that a real Person, Christ, here and now, in that very room where you are saying your prayers, is doing things to you. It is not a question of a good man who died two thousand years ago. It is a living Man, still as much a man as you, and still as much God as He was when He created the world, really coming and interfering with your very self; killing the old natural self in you and replacing it

with the kind of self He has. At first, only for
moments. Then for longer periods. Finally, if all goes
well, turning you permanently into a different sort
of thing; into a new little Christ, a being which, in its
own small way, has the same kind of life as God;
which shares in His power, joy, knowledge and
eternity.[4]

God's word is sharp—sharper than a sword or any razor.
God's word has power to cut and to heal. This is not to
say that the writings of the great philosophers and
theologians and playwrights cannot effect historical
change. Indeed, philosophic paradigms, theological vision
and artistic wisdom have changed the course of personal
and corporate lives. But this is due both to the truth of
what is said and to the ability of the reader to appropriate
the presented wisdom. In the case of God's word, the
element of transcendence is at hand. As we ponder the
words of Christ, it is the Lord himself who is the potter
and we are clay. In the realm of Christian conversion, no
pottery is self-constructed, no matter how profound its
artistry. At times God will use the writings of Plato or
Rahner or Shakespeare to begin the process, but in the
end it is God's word, indeed God's Word, that effects our
fundamental conversion.

Consider: *What sayings of Christ have most radically altered
your attitudes and behavior?*

Thomas Merton (1915-1968) exemplifies a person keenly
aware of his false self. In his correspondence he would
describe himself as a fake, a phony, a hypocrite. With
courageous candor he writes about the struggles of
conversion, how he tried time and again to thwart the
intrusions of grace. We all find it so hard to die to the old
self, to allow God to transform us at our deepest levels.
Fear is a major factor in our resistance as is a lack of trust

and faith. But God never gives up and Merton's journey is a record of God making Merton into "a different sort of thing."

Consider: *How does God interrupt your journey? Are you "a different sort of thing" today than you were ten years ago?*

For Reflection

Conversion means a sharing in the life of God. The foe becomes a friend, the rebel turns obedient, the prodigal is back at table. Now all is different as God shares divine peace, joy, knowledge and eternity with us. Jesus no longer calls us servants but friends, individuals who know his message and participate in the life of the Spirit. Step by step, day by day, we move more deeply into the intimacy of God's love and become increasingly involved in the work of salvation. Though the old self periodically emerges, the light is greater than the darkness, and peace is the gift tasted. How do you collaborate in God's creative designs?

Closing Prayer

"[Religious conversion] dismantles and abolishes the horizon in which our knowing and choosing went on and it sets us a new horizon in which the love of God will transvalue our values and the eyes of that love will transform our knowing."

—Bernard Lonergan

Lord, we hear your call to repent
and follow in your way.
Help us to yield to your passionate desire
that we be your people, agents of your love and
    mercy.
Only your Spirit can empower us to convert,
to turn from darkness to light,
to abolish our narcissism and to live for you.
Conversion is surrender to your will.
Grant us this grace in your mercy. Amen. Alleluia.

Notes

[1] *Surprised by Joy*, pp. 337-338.

[2] A. N. Wilson, *C. S. Lewis: A Biography* (New York: Fawcett Columbine, 1990), p. 126.

[3] *Mere Christianity*, pp. 185-186.

[4] *Mere Christianity*, p. 164.

DAY FOUR

Searchers in the Land of Narnia
Truth

Coming Together in the Spirit

C. S. Lewis was committed to the truth. As a teacher and scholar, his mission in life was to transmit to his hearers the truth that he acquired through study, prayer and serious reflection upon the human experience. As a Christian apologist, Lewis was deeply concerned about handing on the faith to a world that, for the most part, turned away from God and a world that no longer believed in the possibility of truth. Skepticism and relativism impeded confidence in apprehending truth.

Glancing back upon his own history, Lewis was keenly aware of the power of narrative in presenting the truth of things. A good story well told could provide a vision of life that would lead to meaning and commitment. Perhaps this would be the route to communicate the gospel story of salvation in Jesus Christ. Perhaps by writing a story to children Lewis might educate the adult world in matters of faith.

In a seven-volume series—*The Lion, the Witch, and the Wardrobe* (1950), *Prince Caspian* (1951), *The Voyage of the Dawn Treader* (1952), *The Silver Chair* (1953), *The Horse and His Boy* (1954), *The Magician's Nephew* (1955), *The Last Battle* (1956)—known as *The Chronicles of Narnia*, C. S. Lewis constructs an intricate narrative involving the redemption of the world through the self-giving love of Aslan (the mighty lion). He explores the mystery of evil and sin through the adventures of Digory Kirke and the wickedness of the White Witch. And he portrays the self-giving love of God bringing life where before there was death, through the adventures of four children—Peter, Edmund, Susan and Lucy Pevensey.

The Chronicles of Narnia are about truth and falsity, goodness and evil, beauty and ugliness. We encounter talking animals, magical wands, distortions of time and space—and truth, the truth about ourselves and life. No one can venture through the door of the wardrobe and return the same. No one can encounter Aslan and ever again not know the mercy of God.

Defining Our Thematic Context

On this fourth day of retreat we will listen to the wisdom and truth of Aslan who came to give his life for the children (and the world) and thereby set all of us free, free to worship now without fear.

Opening Prayer

God of truth and love,
you speak to us in word and sacrament,
in the richness of our tradition,
in the creativity of the human heart,
always to draw us into the truth of your light,
always to call us to the beauty of your love.
In the story of Genesis we ponder the truth of
    creation,
the devastation of sin, the promise of new life.

In the stories of Christian writers we hear told again
the ways of grace and the detours of sin.
Send your Spirit to enlighten our minds
so that guided by your truth, by whatever channel it
    comes to us,
we may glorify your name and walk always in
    freedom as your children.

RETREAT SESSION FOUR

We reflect first on whether truth is safe or good. In
volume one of the *Chronicles*, *The Lion, the Witch, and the
Wardrobe*, the four Pevensey children have miraculously
entered the land of Narnia through a secret door in a
wardrobe. Lost and afraid and pursued, they encounter
some talking beavers who offer the children hospitality,
and more. Mr. Beaver makes mention of a character
known as Aslan. Listen prayerfully to this dialogue.

"Who is Aslan?" asked Susan.
"Aslan?" said Mr. Beaver, "Why don't you know?
He's the King... It is he, not you, that will save Mr.
Tumnus...."
"Is—is he a man?" asked Lucy.
"Aslan a man!" said Mr. Beaver sternly.
"Certainly not. I tell you he is the King of the wood
and the son of the great Emperor-Beyond-the-Sea.
Don't you know who is the King of Beasts? Aslan is
a lion—the Lion, the great Lion."
"Ooh!" said Susan. "I'd thought he was a man. Is
he—quite safe? I shall feel rather nervous about
meeting a lion."
"That you will, dearie, and no mistake," said Mrs.
Beaver, "if there's anyone who can appear before

Aslan without their knees knocking, they're either braver than most or else just silly."

"Then he isn't safe?" said Lucy.

"Safe?" said Mr. Beaver. "Don't you hear what Mrs. Beaver tells you? Who said anything about safe? 'Course he isn't safe. But he's good. He's the King, I tell you."

"I'm longing to see him," said Peter, "even if I do feel frightened when it comes to the point."[1]

Truth confronts our ignorance: "Don't you know...?" All the way through the gospel we see the constant ignorance of the crowds and of the disciples in their failure to understand who Jesus was and why he came. The truth escaped them for a variety of reasons: stupidity, blindness, fear of knowing, narcissism and the list goes on. Jesus eventually poses the question: "Who do you say that I am?" Faith leads to a variety of answers: Messiah, Son of God, Savior, Redeemer, Friend. Like the children in Narnia, the gradual revelation of Aslan, the Lion of Judah, took time and led to a knowledge that came only by way of suffering and pain. Finding the truth about the mystery of Christ is never theoretical. It is always experiential and demanding.

Consider: *If you were given ten minutes to summarize your knowledge of Jesus, what would you say?*

Truth is not safe but it is good. Security and safety are treasured values in our day. Our nature rebels against circumstances that make us insecure and put us at risk. Yet the journey of faith does not guarantee safety, only the promise of God's presence. The truth of the matter is that God is good and is trustworthy. But throwing in our lot with Christ means that we are willing to walk his path and that the road to Calvary is never safe. In the land of Narnia the young children must learn to have courage if they are to adhere to the truth. Both are graces; both are gifts that God promises to those who ask in faith. Aslan is a good lion, willing to give his life for others, but he is not safe in the sense that we will become immune to suffering if we hold on to his mane.

Consider: *Do you value the proverb: "Better safe than sorry"? Or are you willing to risk and suffer if thereby you come to the truth of things?*

Truth is so deep a human need that it creates a perpetual longing. When Peter hears about the great Lion from the evangelizing beavers, a longing arises within his heart that is so deep that even terrible fears cannot still the yearning to see Aslan. The fourth grade student who hears about great explorers feels something stir within his or her young soul, a something that smells of adventure and release from the imprisonment of the classroom. Peter responds to the very mystery of Aslan's name, a name that carried the energy of hope and salvation and freedom. Contrary wants—for comfort, safety, security—were no match for the powerful longing induced by the anticipated presence of Aslan. In this Lion the truth would be revealed and the children set free.

Consider: *What were some of your first real, deep longings? What names did you assign to them?*

Turning to the theme of our spiritual search for truth we see that in *The Silver Chair*, the Narnia story continues as two young children, Eustace Scrub and Jill Pole, are brought by Aslan to Narnia to search for a long-lost prince. While on that journey Jill is dying of thirst and encounters Aslan who stands between her and some life-giving water. Here is the dialogue:

"Are you not thirsty?" said the Lion.

"I'm dying of thirst," said Jill.

"Then drink," said the Lion.

"May I—could I—would you mind going away while I do?" said Jill.

The Lion answered this only by a look and a very low growl. And as Jill gazed at its motionless bulk, she realized that she might as well have asked the whole mountain to move aside for her convenience. The delicious rippling noise of the stream was driving her near frantic.

"Will you promise not to—to do anything to me, if I do come?" said Jill.

"I make no promise," said the Lion.

Jill was so thirsty now that, without noticing it, she had come a step nearer.

"Do you eat girls?" she said.

"I have swallowed up girls and boys, women and men, kings and emperors, cities and realms," said the Lion. It didn't say this as if it were boasting, nor as if it were sorry, nor as if it were angry. It just said it.

"I daren't come and drink," said Jill.

"Then you will die of thirst," said the Lion.

"Oh, dear!" said Jill, coming another step nearer. "I suppose I must go and look for another stream then."

"There is no other stream," said the Lion.[2]

There are truths and then there is Truth. Christianity makes a bold claim in its assertion that it is in Christ Jesus that salvation is found: "There is no other stream." Jesus is the way into the mystery of God since he is the manifestation of God's love, compassion and forgiveness. This proposition demands careful nuancing. Millions, even billions, of people over the long course of human history have never known the historical Jesus. Yet all life and all holiness comes to us through Christ in the Holy

Spirit. Christ is involved in the very mystery of creation and through this life-giving event becomes the stream that nourishes and sustains life. Jesus is the way, the truth and the life.

Consider: *What paths do you follow in seeking the stream that is Christ?*

Truth cannot be bargained with; it has its own integrity. Often the truth is difficult to bear, its blinding light revealing every facet of our lives. Perhaps we might be given life and grace without having to confront the Source of these blessings. Such is not to be. God does not "go away" but abides with us until we become true daughters and sons. Compromise is not found in God's lexicon. Yet in all this, God's timing is exquisite and we are never given the whole truth until the time is ripe.

Consider: *How has God revealed you to yourself?*

Truth is a matter of life and death. Aslan is direct with Jill. If Jill or any of us do not drink from the living spring of grace we will die. Our spiritual lives must be nourished with the truth of God's love and forgiveness. In *The Chronicles of Narnia*, Aslan is the one who gives his life for others and brings the dead back to life. There is no power other than the mystery of such love that can satisfy the human spirit. Without Aslan the kingdom of Narnia is under the dominion of the White Witch who brings coldness and death to all the inhabitants of Narnia. With the coming of Aslan comes spring and with it life and hope. With Aslan comes the truth that life is stronger than death.

Consider: *Why does truth matter so much? Does it matter even more than love?*

We turn now to truth, our true homeland. In *The Voyage of the "Dawn Treader,"* there is a major quest to find Aslan's country. During this vast sea journey, Edmund and Lucy Pevensey are joined by Reepicheep, a mouse, on this high adventure. Here is a scene in which Lucy and Edmund meet Aslan disguised as a lamb. The children are seeking the way into Aslan's country:

> But between them and the foot of the sky there was something so white on the green grass that even with their eagles' eyes they could hardly look at it. They came on and saw that it was a Lamb.
>
> "Come and have breakfast," said the Lamb in its sweet milky voice....
>
> "Please, Lamb," said Lucy, "is this the way to Aslan's country?"
>
> "Not for you," said the Lamb. "For you the door into Aslan's country is from your own world."
>
> "What!" said Edmund. "Is there a way into Aslan's country from our world too?"
>
> "There is a way into my country from all the worlds," said the Lamb; but as he spoke his snowy white flushed into tawny gold and his size changed and he was Aslan himself, towering above them and scattering light from his mane.
>
> "Oh, Aslan," said Lucy. "Will you tell us how to get into your country from our world?"
>
> "I shall be telling you all the time," said Aslan. "But I will not tell you how long or short the way will be; only that it lies across a river. But do not fear that, for I am the great Bridge Builder. And now come; I will open the door in the sky and send you to your own land."[3]

God's truth is often disguised and comes to us in surprising ways. In the Gospels we read how the risen Christ keeps appearing to his fearful disciples under various disguises: a gardener, a pilgrim, a cook. God keeps accommodating divine light to the circumstances of the human spirit. In the above quotation, Lucy and Edmund meet the Lamb/Lion. They fail to recognize that in this encounter they are already in the country that they are so desperately seeking. Aslan is home. The country sought is God's presence with all its light, love and joy.

Consider: *How does the risen Lord break into your life?*

It is a basic truth that there is a way or door into God's kingdom from all worlds. One of the characteristics of our age is diversity: diversity of cultures, languages, life-styles. Our global village, through modern communication, exposes us to a multiplicity of worlds. God is present throughout all creation, and grace is working in every land and every human heart. Whether or not this truth is recognized and responded to depends upon numerous factors, the most important being human freedom. But the point is: Whatever the world, God is there and can be encountered. Every moment presents an opportunity for getting into Aslan's country, the country of light, love and life.

Consider: *What are the major elements in your world? The people, the symbols, the themes, the questions? Where is grace operative in these elements?*

In all times and in all places, God constructs bridges for our passage into his country. Sometimes the bridge connecting us to God's presence is a song, or a poem, or a piece of art work, or a season of the year. These "bridges," these circumstances are portals through which we travel from darkness to light, from death to life, from fear to trust. Obviously they are not made of steel and concrete. Rather, they are subtle forces that draw us down the road of conversion. For Lucy and Edmund, the wardrobe began their adventure into Aslan's country. But God is constantly calling us into the divine presence so that we might have life and life to the full.

Consider: *What has been the most important bridge giving you entrance into God's presence?*

For Reflection

Pilate raised the question that haunts every generation: "What is truth?" Each person and each culture must respond to this inquiry. The skeptic rejects truth as unattainable; the rationalist relies on reasoning to achieve it; the believer assents to God's revelation. C. S. Lewis traveled all of these roads, as many of us have done. His legacy in the realm of truth for children is the lion Aslan. In this "character," good but not safe, kind but demanding, self-giving but terrifying, we are given a picture, not a concept of truth. Would that adults could apprehend this truth as easily as children. To reflect further, reread *The Lion, the Witch, and the Wardrobe*.

Closing Prayer

"Truth is like a vast tree, which yields more and more fruit the more you nurture it. The deeper the search in the mine of truth the richer the discovery of the gems buried there, in the shape of opening for an ever greater variety of service."
—Gandhi

God of truth,
you pursue us "down the nights and down the days,"
longing that we yield and surrender our minds to
    your wisdom.
Help us to see;
grant us insight and knowledge
into what is truly important in light.
Send Aslan into our lives.
We ask this in Jesus' name.

Notes

[1] C. S. Lewis, *The Lion, the Witch, and the Wardrobe* (New York: Macmillan, 1970), pp. 74-76.

[2] C. S. Lewis, *The Silver Chair* (New York: Macmillan, 1970), pp. 16-17.

[3] C. S. Lewis, *The Voyage of the "Dawn Treader"* (New York: Macmillan, 1970), pp. 214-215.

DAY FIVE

Till We Have Faces and Voices
Identity

Coming Together in the Spirit

In 1956, Lewis wrote a complex work *Till We Have Faces*, a retelling of the ancient Greek myth about Cupid and Psyche. It is a story of adventure in which the two central characters, Queen Orual and her half-sister Psyche, struggle in their relationship. This difficult novel takes place in remote times, deals with imaginary lands and barbaric kings, contends with deities that require of humans impossible things.

Inside the narrative there are several basic questions: What is authentic love in contrast to possessiveness? What are the limits of reason and why is the imagination so powerful? How can we go through the process of "undeception" so that we come to know our true face and find our authentic voice? It's a story about atonement for wrong done and about the redemptive act of taking another's place in their suffering and grief. It's a human story told under the guise of mythology.

Defining Our Thematic Context

Retreat is a time to look into the heart of God and also into the mirror to see if we are imaging our God. Retreat gives us pause to ask if we speak out of conviction and commitment or whether we are merely mouthing speeches and lines from someone else's play. C. S. Lewis consistently raises the fundamental questions about identity, love and salvation. It is in Christ and the life that he lived that we come to know to whom we belong and what life is all about.

Opening Prayer

God, our creator, redeemer and sanctifier, you call us to be your people and to do your work.

You have given us the awesome gift of freedom, a grace filled with power and ambiguity.

We have no choice but to make choices; we have no freedom but to decide on life or death.

Send your Spirit of wisdom into our minds that we might know "whose" we are; send your Spirit of reverence into our hearts that we might discern your call.

Until we have self-knowledge, we will never know you our creator and redeemer; until we have found our own voice, we will not speak your word well.

We praise you for calling us into existence and we thank you for establishing your covenant.

May we grow in grace this day and every day of our life.

RETREAT SESSION FIVE

We begin by reflecting on identity: the center of our souls. One way we come to an understanding and, hopefully, acceptance of our identity is through the use of language. We strive to find words to describe what lies at the core of our very being. No easy task here. Our inner lives are so complex and our outer circumstances so multiple that it takes tremendous effort and focused determination to arrive at some clarity regarding our self-identity. Saint Augustine once held that "...joy in truth is the happy life." As Lewis observes, when our words are true we come close to the edge of joy and happiness:

> The complaint was the answer. To have heard myself making it was to be answered. Lightly men talk of saying what they mean. Often when he was teaching me to write in Greek the Fox would say, "Child, to say the very things you really mean, the whole of it, nothing more or less or other than what you really mean; that's the whole art and joy of words." A glib saying. When the time comes to you at which you will be forced at last to utter the speech which has lain at the center of your soul for years, which you have, all that time, idiot-like, been saying over and over, you'll not talk about the joy of words. I saw well why the gods do not speak to us, openly, nor let us answer. Till that word can be dug out of us, why should they hear the babble that we think we mean? How can they meet us face to face till we have faces?[1]

Identity is wrapped up in meaning, and meaning comes to light in words. How difficult it is to say what we really mean. How difficult it is to express the very meaning of our being. Part of our existence is ideal, our dream of what we ought to be. So we find words to express our ambitions and our wishes. Another part of our life is our social role, wherein we take on the identity of parent, professor, nurse, farmer, engineer. But then we are challenged to go deep into our souls, beyond our ideal and social selves, to the real "me." This journey is long and tortuous, demanding great courage and prayerful insight. What a grace to arrive at the level of communication by which we accurately say what our true meaning is.

Consider: *What words do you use to describe your ideal, social and real self?*

Is there such a thing as the joy of words, or, the sorrow of words? I believe there is. Words are bearers of thoughts, feelings, activities, indeed, of our very self. They are messengers performing an invaluable task of bringing to light that which lies hidden. Joy happens when our speech is true and authentic, even if painful; sorrow is found in words that relay news of sadness and tragedy. God speaks to us through the Scriptures and especially in the Word, Jesus. When we hear that Word and respond to it with true obedience, we come to our true identity and to authentic freedom.

Consider: *What words of Scripture help you to know your true identity? Isaiah 43?*

Retreat is a time of prayer, a communication in which God speaks to us and we speak to our God. In order for dialogue to happen there is one thing that is absolutely necessary: we must bring "this me," my real self, my real face, my real voice, to the living and true God. If we approach an imaginary God—some harsh judge or transcendent dictator—or if we enter God's presence with a disguised voice or a countenance not our own, nothing will happen. The intimacy of prayer demands an encounter with reality. Till we have faces and voices that are truly our own, we remain distant from a loving and merciful God.

Consider: *How has your prayer life grown in the last five years?*

Our second theme today is: Who are we, or *whose* are we? Formulating a well-ordered question is a special art. The way the question is asked sets a framework for the answer. In dealing with the issue of identity we might ask the question that fosters a false autonomy: Who am I? Easily enough we say doctor, lawyer, banker, chef. But to ask "whose are we" sets the tone of relationships. My identity comes from my relationship that involves giving myself to someone or something, be it God, my own ego, pleasure, power, greed or lust. In the novel *Till We Have Faces* there is a constant pondering of "Whose am I?"

Lewis addresses the happiness and identity question in another text, *Mere Christianity*, in which he writes:

> God designed the human machine to run on Himself. He Himself is the fuel our spirits were designed to burn, or the food our spirits were designed to feed on. There is no other. That is why it is just no good asking God to make us happy in our own way without bothering about religion. God cannot give us a happiness and peace apart from Himself, because it is not there. There is no such thing.[2]

At a gathering this summer we were asked at table what is our "soul food." What is the fuel and food that nourishes our relationship with God and keeps our souls vibrant and growing? The answers were diverse: personal prayer, fasting, ministry, walking in nature, spiritual reading, counseling or direction, and the list went on. All agreed that our spiritual lives needed specific and disciplined attention if we were to be true to our deepest self, if we were to achieve the task of finding our voice and discovering our true countenance. We also discussed the obstacles that hindered the discovery and expression of our authentic identity. Things like procrastination, imbalance, activism, lack of priorities. There was no disagreement regarding our need for daily nourishment to stay spiritually healthy.

Consider: *What is your favorite "soul food"? What causes you spiritual indigestion?*

Is happiness possible without God, without religion? Contemporary authors have long lists and menus that promise happiness: control, self-esteem, achievable goals, friendship, satisfying work. Always in the background is that haunting line from the very first chapter of Augustine's *Confessions*: "For Thou has made us for Thyself and our hearts are restless till they rest in Thee."[3] We are constructed in a certain way; we are made for infinity. Nothing finite can ultimately satisfy our souls. It may well be that our national sin is one of "unbridled restlessness," a restlessness that we seek to placate by means of blatant consumerism, rampant individualism, excessive workism. In the end we come back to our existential indigence and our poverty of spirit. Only God can give us happiness and our true identity.

Consider: *How do you deal with your restlessness? Any major compensatory behaviors?*

The question of finding our voice, discovering our face, knowing who we really are ultimately leads us to the issue of peace. In what lies that rightness of relationships, that incredible congruence that we call peace? The poet Gerard Manley Hopkins offers us one person's search for this elusive wood dove, this grace we call peace:

Peace

When will you ever, Peace, wildwood dove, shy
   wings shut,

Your round me roaming end, and under be my
    boughs?
When, when, Peace, will you, Peace? I'll not play
    hypocrite

To own my heart: I yield you do come sometimes; but
That piecemeal peace is poor peace. What pure peace
    allows
Alarms of wars, the daunting wars, the death of it?

O surely, reaving Peace, my Lord should leave in lieu
Some good! And so he does leave Patience exquisite,
That plumes to Peace thereafter. And when Peace
    here does house
He comes with work to do, he does not come to coo,
He comes to brood and sit.[4]

Hopkins describes anything apart from God as
"piecemeal peace"—"poor peace." The heart and soul
long for pure peace, that faith relationship that nothing,
not even suffering and death, can destroy. But given the
human condition and the succession of time, we are in a
constant state of tension as we deal with this thing we call
our spiritual life. Though "piecemeal peace" is never
satisfactory, we must make do and trust that fullness will
come in the risen life.

Consider: *What has been one of the most "peaceful" phases of
your faith journey?*

Every good story is about people changing. In Lewis's *Till
We Have Faces* we can see ourselves as if in a mirror as the
various characters are confronted with life-determining
decisions, relationships that bring joy or strain,
circumstances that call for active response or patient
endurance. All of us are on the road to becoming,
becoming what God intends us to be: instruments and

channels of truth, love and goodness. One of the great
enigmas of life deals with the polarities of activity and
passivity in our lives. What is our degree of responsibility
in determining the quality of our character, what is our
situation in being shaped and molded by a creative God?
In reflecting on the notion of personhood, C. S. Lewis
makes this statement:

> We shall then first be true persons when we have
> suffered ourselves to be fitted into our places. We
> are marble waiting to be shaped, metal waiting to be
> run into a mould.[5]

In writing about the weakness of utilitarian ethics, Albert
Schweitzer claimed that this form of morality was unable
to integrate half of the ethical life: enduring what comes
to us—things we do not control. Certainly we are to be
proactive in the shaping of our identity and destiny.
Freedom is the faculty by which we exercise some control
over the circumstances and relationships of our lives.
However, there is much that is beyond our control. We
suffer things, endure periods of painful waiting, are
challenged to be open to the molding forces of history
and the continuing creative action of God. Jeremiah the
prophet images God as the potter (Jeremiah 18) and us as
the clay. We are not our own masters, though we must
exercise appropriate responsibility when the situation
demands it.

Consider: *Are you more comfortable with the active or passive
dimensions of your life? Why?*

Becoming our true self is a lifelong process. A tension
continuously plagues us as we are challenged to repeat the
voices of the past—parents, tradition, church, history—
and yet feel deeply the urge to personal integrity and self-
development. Like other tensions in life (time/eternity,

free/determined, body/soul) it is never either/or. Our voices should repeat the truths of the past while articulating contemporary wisdom we extract from our own personal experience. There is something unique and significant that we are to contribute to history and those contributions will not be made without becoming the unique person God calls us to be. Walt Whitman found his voice and sang his unique poetic songs. So, too, did Lena Horne and Jimmy Stewart and Pope John Paul II. We follow Jesus not by some slavish imitation but by doing what he did: speaking in his own voice the words given him by the Father.

Consider: *In the past five years, what has your unique voice contributed to the world?*

Analogies are helpful in discovering new meanings and deeper insights into life. They are also limiting in that they cannot say everything and must necessarily leave out even essential elements. C. S. Lewis is a master teacher, especially in his use of analogy. He states that we are marble and metal, waiting to be shaped, waiting to be poured into a mold. Yes and no. God's creative hand is always shaping us just as the divine Breath moves within us. Yet the analogy does highlight the need to cooperate in the faces we are to wear, the voices we are to speak. Perhaps this comparison might capture the role of our participation in this process of becoming. We are like a sunflower which is gifted with sunlight and rain, nutrients from the earth and assistance from the gardener. But all must be freely appropriated and transformed into a unique plant, a unique person. It is precisely in cooperation with this freedom, when exercised with responsibility, that we find our voice and form our countenance.

Consider: *What analogy helps you to understand the process of becoming the person God wants you to be?*

For Reflection

In *Till We Have Faces*, Lewis explores the doctrine of "exchange" based on the Great Exchange made by God in Christ: the Incarnation and the cross. He believed that through Christian love one person could accept into his or her own body the pain of another. Lewis put this belief into practice by praying for and receiving the gift of easing his wife's suffering from cancer by experiencing her pain himself. To reflect on the theme of the redemptive power of sacrificial love, read the closing scene of *Till We Have Faces*.

Closing Prayer

"For, though I speak it to you, I think the King is but a man, as I am. The violet smells to him as it doth to me; the element shows to him as it doth to me; all his senses have but human condition."

—William Shakespeare,
Henry V, Act IV, Scene 1

Gracious God,
is it possible that we are made to your image and
likeness,
formed by your hand to become like unto you?
Is our identity found only in our knowledge of who
you are?
Quickly send your Spirit to help us yield to your
truth,

to surrender to your ways,
to say "yes" as Mary did.
Until we do so we will lack our true voice and
    authentic face.
Help us to follow in the way of your son, Jesus.
    Amen. Alleluia.

Notes

[1] C. S. Lewis, *Till We Have Faces* (Grand Rapids, Mich.: Eerdmans, 1966), p. 294.

[2] *Mere Christianity*, p. 54.

[3] *The Confessions of St. Augustine*, trans. by F. J. Sheed (New York: Sheed & Ward, 1943), p. 3.

[4] *Poems of Gerard Manley Hopkins*, ed. by W. H. Gardner and N. H. Mackenzie (New York: Oxford University Press, 1967).

[5] C. S. Lewis, *The Weight of Glory and Other Addresses* (New York: Macmillan, 1980), p. 118.

DAY SIX

The Problem of Pain and Evil
Suffering

Coming Together in the Spirit

It takes considerable courage to sit down and write a
book about suffering. C. S. Lewis had that courage when,
in 1940, he published *The Problem of Pain*. In this small,
challenging volume, Lewis addresses many issues: God's
providence and goodness, the wickedness of humanity,
the realities of heaven and hell, and pain as experienced
by animals and humans. One of the better known lines
from Lewis provides a context for this day of retreat:
"God whispers to us in our pleasures, speaks in our
conscience, but shouts in our pains: it is His megaphone
to rouse a deaf world."

Defining Our Thematic Context

All of us suffer. For some it is the physical pain of a
broken bone in failing to negotiate winter's ice. For others
it is the agonizing pain of depression or mental illness or
ambiguous anxieties that leave us weary and downcast.
For still others, pain criss-crosses the soul and is of a
spiritual nature: the pain of God's absence or the
suffering from a troubled conscience. And, of course, we
might experience all three at various times in our lives. In

faith the question always arises: What is God's role in all of this? Cause? Indifferent Bystander? Compassionate Presence? Wrathful Deity? In prayer we strive to be open to God's word as we deal with the problem of pain.

Opening Prayer

God of wisdom and love, grant us insight into the
    mystery of suffering.
Before the terror of pain and the destructiveness of
    evil, we stand paralyzed, dumbfounded,
    perplexed.
Where does this darkness come from?
Are you in any way a cause of this blackness?
How can we find meaning and purpose in this
    apparent absurdity?
Gracious God, come to our aid.
We are powerless in this valley of pain and lost before
    "the banality of evil."
Reveal to us the mystery of Jesus, your Son, and help
    us understand the events of Calvary.
Only under the cross can we find hope.
Only at the empty tomb can we know faith.
Only through your Presence are we touched by that
    Love which empowers us to accept whatever
    comes.

RETREAT SESSION SIX

Our first meditation theme today is on unsettled happiness. One of my favorite poems is "The Pulley" by George Herbert. The verse narrates how God, in creating

the world and gifting us human beings, gives us many
blessings such as beauty and wisdom and pleasure. But
one thing is withheld: rest! The poet Herbert reasons that
if God were to bestow this tremendous jewel upon the
creature, ultimately both God and the human person
would be losers since we would rest "in Nature, not the
God of nature: / So both should losers be." Though
Herbert does not address the topic of suffering
specifically, the implication is that suffering, too, is a
pulley that draws us back to God. C. S. Lewis and George
Herbert are on the same wavelength:

> The Christian doctrine of suffering explains, I
> believe, a very curious fact about the world we live
> in. The settled happiness and security which we all
> desire, God withholds from us by the very nature of
> the world: but joy, pleasure, and merriment He has
> scattered broadcast. We are never safe, but we have
> plenty of fun, and some ecstasy. It is not hard to see
> why. The security we crave would teach us to rest in
> this world and pose an obstacle to our return to
> God: a few moments of happy love, a landscape, a
> symphony, a merry meeting with friends, a date or a
> football match, have no such tendency. Our Father
> refreshes us on the journey with some pleasant inns,
> but will not encourage us to mistake them for
> home.[1]

Our desire for security and happiness is deep and
abiding. Significant amounts of energy and time are
devoted to their acquisition as many of us strive for
economic independence, a sense of well-being, personal
peace. And rightly so. Insecurity causes anxiety and
unhappiness often leads to unproductive lives. Yet there
is a deeper hunger and thirst in our spirit that transcends
basic security and personal happiness. We are made for
God and all too easily we choose a lesser reality: a big
home, prestige at the office or university, pleasures of

food and drink. Idolatry is still capable of being our national and personal sin. C. S. Lewis was convinced that God withholds from us a settled security and happiness, not because of indifference or hatred, but out of love. Our restlessness, no small pain and suffering, will keep us on the journey and the road to eternal joy.

Consider: *How do you seek security and happiness? Have these become idols in your life?*

Making people feel important and giving them a sense of safety are two values that we hold dear. Yet we are never safe. Life, by its very nature, is precarious. We do not know from one moment to the next whether we will continue in existence. An earthquake, a plane crash, a heart attack and everything is changed. Yet life holds so many joys and moments of ecstasy: falling in love, gaining new insight, watching a golden sunset, singing and dancing our traditions. These diverse forms of refreshment help us to continue the journey and bear the burdens of life. Yet a radical poverty permeates our human existence, the mystery of which involves pain and suffering. Faith is the grace needed to accept our human condition and to find God in the midst of travail. Though our physical and psychological safety is never secured, faith does give us assurance that God is with us every step of the way.

Consider: *How do you make others feel important and safe?*

In dealing with the issue of pain and suffering, it is crucial that we retain a sense of eschatology, an awareness of the last things. Lewis reminds us that this planet is not our lasting home. We came from God and are destined for God. This sense of the last things (heaven, hell) puts our lives in perspective, including our suffering and pain. For some death does come as a blessing in that chronic pain is ended. Suffering, when redemptive, can serve as a reminder that there is more to life than our daily work and pleasures. The challenge is to unite our suffering with Christ's, so that as we share in his passion we, too, shall share in his Resurrection and experience the joy of everlasting life.

Consider: *What helps you to stay conscious of the eschatological dimensions of your faith life?*

Now we turn our attention to "Suffering and Divine Humility." It is not surprising that Rabbi Harold Kushner's book *Why Bad Things Happen to Good People* was a best-seller. Good people—decent, inoffensive, honorable folks—often experience tragedy which they do not deserve. It is at this intersection—between a good God and the suffering of innocent people—that the soul is thrown into confusion. No one has articulated an answer that is satisfactory. Confronted with this mystery the mind reaches its limits and even the heart is perplexed. The only exit here is to see how many innocent, suffering people embrace their sufferings with as much grace as they embrace the blessings of their lives.

> We are perplexed to see misfortune falling upon decent, inoffensive, worthy people...God, who made these deserving people, may really be right when He thinks that their modest prosperity and the happiness of their children are not enough to make them blessed: that all this must fall from them in the end, and that if they have not learned to know Him they will be wretched. And therefore he troubles them, warning them in advance of an insufficiency that one day they will have to discover. The life to themselves and their family stands between them and the recognition of the need; He makes that life less sweet to them. I call this a Divine humility

> because it is a poor thing to strike our colours to
> God when the ship is going down under us; a poor
> thing to come to Him as a last resort, to offer up
> "our own" when it is no longer worth keeping. If
> God were proud He would hardly have us on such
> terms; but He is not proud, He stoops to conquer,
> He will have us even though we have shown that
> we prefer everything else to Him, and come to Him
> because there is "nothing better" now to be had.[2]

In what does happiness consist? One schema includes
such things as a positive self-image, sufficient financial
resources, a good education, reasonable liberties,
supportive friendships. From a faith perspective,
happiness is linked to our relationship with God: a
deeper knowing and loving. These capacities can remain
atrophied and underdeveloped because of our
preoccupation with things and even personal
relationships. There is no time for "transcendence," for
the things of God. It can happen that an experience of
tragedy and suffering can awaken us to the central
matters of existence. Our other values, important as they
seem, are stripped away and, in our painful nakedness,
we encounter the mystery of God.

Consider: *What is your working definition of happiness? Its
central components?*

The story of the prodigal son (Luke 15) is a parable about
the humility of God. The younger son squandered his
inheritance and abandoned his family. Then the suffering
came, self-imposed by a life-style that was destructive. But
the son still had some sense. He would return, empty-
handed and empty-hearted, and seek forgiveness. God,
like the father in the story, is moved with compassion and
we are familiar with his joy at the son's return. This story
is the human story of giftedness, squandering, suffering,

reconciliation, forgiveness. In contrast to the arrogance and hurt of the elder son, we seek to know how powerful Divine humility is. God, being love, cannot refuse to love.

Consider: *What is the relationship between suffering and squandering in your life?*

A key issue in our day, and perhaps in every age, is the question of sufficiency, the question of enoughness. The Latin word *satis* means enough, thus satisfaction is the condition in which we have had enough: enough food, enough money, enough power, enough pleasure. Our times are restless and there is a constant desire for more. In this there is a suffering and pain that is filled with anxiety. Associated with this is envy and jealousy, two capital sins. We are like a pitcher with a hole in the bottom. No matter how much water or wine is poured in, there is never enough because it is leaking out. Suffering and deprivation ends when the pitcher is immersed in the river or wine vat. Only in God do we find our peace.

Consider: *Is "enough" an operative word in your lexicon?*

Our closing theme is suffering with Christ. In Jesus our God has experienced suffering and pain from the inside. Though divine, Jesus embraced the surrender and humiliation that is part of the human journey. The Scriptures inform us that if we share in the Lord's suffering and death, we will participate in the Resurrection, the new life given us in Jesus. In no way is our suffering lessened, but now it is set in a context that removes absolute absurdity. Lewis states:

> The perfect surrender and humiliation were undergone by Christ: perfect because He was God, surrender and humiliation because He was man. Now the Christian belief is that if we somehow

share the humility and suffering of Christ we shall
also share in His conquest of death and find a new
life after we have died and in it become perfect, and
perfectly happy, creatures. This means something
much more than our trying to follow His teaching.
People often ask when the next step in evolution—
the step to something beyond man—will happen.
But in the Christian view, it has happened already.
In Christ a new kind of man appeared: and the new
kind of life which began in Him is to be put into us.

One of the current principles that drives effective people
is being proactive. The challenge here is to make things
happen, take charge, maintain control, so that specific
ends can be accomplished. But there is another dimension
in life that lies at the heart of suffering and pain:
endurance. This is the land of surrender and humiliation,
experienced on a daily basis by those who, because of
circumstances or sometimes choice, no longer have
control. Jesus was proactive in fulfilling the mission given
him by the Father. But a significant part of the divine plan
involved a Gethsemane surrender and a Calvary
humiliation. The fact that our God experienced these
fundamental human experiences should fill us with hope.

Consider: *What is your response to moments of humiliation
and the invitation to surrender your will?*

Christian spirituality, by definition, means participation, a
sharing in the life of God. Another basic principle in life is
that "growth demands participation." And this type of
sharing cannot be selective. We share in the whole of
Jesus' journey, the ecstasy of the Jordan baptism, the
adventure of being called and sent, the pain of total self-
surrender. Belief is not enough; faith is demanded. We
need to have that radical conviction that through Jesus'
death a new life flows. We are challenged to embrace the

paradox that an apparently failed mission was in fact an incredible success. The Paschal Mystery has once and for all confounded our contemporary value system. Now death leads to life, failure to success, humiliation to glory.

Consider: *How deeply do you participate in the mystery of the Eucharist?*

I've heard tell that a hospital in the Bible belt requires that new admitted patients not only record the day of their birth, but also the date of their rebirth. Saint Paul would not find this difficult for he knew the exact date and place of his rebirth in Jesus. Grace, the gift of God's very life given in Jesus, plunges us into a new river in which the currents of compassion and mercy and love carry us along. It is a new life, a new kind of life that defies description and that demands experience. For those who have not accepted this whole new life it can no more be explained to them than colors to a person without sight. Just as physical birth involves considerable pain in the passage from one location to another, so in the spiritual realm. Surrender and abandonment are costly sacrifices.

Consider: *Can you record the date of your rebirth? Was it a gradual or sudden process?*

For Reflection

The opening sentence of Lewis's *A Grief Observed* is: "No one ever told me that grief felt so like fear." Recall your own experiences of grief. If you choose, read Matthew 14:3-13 and consider what emotions Jesus may have struggled with after the death of his herald. What might he have feared? Write a brief personal reflection on the relationship between grief and fear.

Closing Prayer

"There are no frontiers between suffering people...."
—Etty Hillesum

God of humility,
you embrace in Jesus our human suffering,
and hunt us even in the fields of pain and death.
May we yield to your poverty and embrace our cross
as a way of living always in your love.
We do not understand this great mystery.
Send your Spirit that at least we might say yes
to your way of salvation.
Grant this through the humble, suffering Savior.
    Amen. Alleluia.

Notes

[1] C. S. Lewis, *The Problem of Pain* (New York: Macmillan, 1962), p. 115.

[2] *The Problem of Pain*, pp. 96-97.

DAY SEVEN

Observing a Grief
Death

Coming Together in the Spirit

C. S. Lewis consistently took his daily experience and brought it to that creative workshop of "process." No doubt he held with conviction that old adage: "Experiences unreflected upon dehumanize." Thus when his wife Joy died, Lewis had to find words to deal with the anguish and grief that tore through his heart. He had to process her death and his loss as best he could and he did this by entering notes into four exercise books. The result was published in *A Grief Observed* (1961), originally under the pseudonym, N. W. Clerk.

The contrast between this work and his early writings on suffering and death, *The Problem of Pain* (1940), is remarkable, though not surprising. *A Grief Observed* is intensely personal, existential, heart-rending; *The Problem of Pain* is abstract, quite impersonal and highly cognitive. In one, the author is a major participant; in the other, a somewhat distant observer. Lewis courageously attempted to offer insight into two of the greatest mysteries of life: suffering and death. We owe him a debt of gratitude for his wisdom.

Defining Our Thematic Context

Our contemporary culture has been labeled a number of things: a culture of complaint, a culture of greed, and yes, a culture of death. Violence has overwhelmed our world community causing destruction and death in its undiscriminating path. Laws are in place permitting doctors to terminate the life of the unborn and laws are being contemplated allowing assisted suicide. Death surrounds us and can become so ubiquitous as to deaden our ability to mourn. C. S. Lewis assists us in facing the mystery of death and helps us to respond appropriately to its haunting reality.

Opening Prayer

God of the living and the dead,
you who call us to fullness of life,
enlighten us to understand the mystery of death.
Before this grave door we stand unknowing,
before this dark enigma we stand trembling.
Loss of our loved ones fills us with grief,
our own "loss" causes us great anxiety.
Give us the vision of your son Jesus
that we might follow him through the mystery
    of the cross
into the glory of your kingdom.
Let not our fear impede our faith,
let not our ignorance block our hope.
Come, Lord of the living and the dead,
and turn our grief to joy.

RETREAT SESSION SEVEN

Let's begin our final session by considering death a test of faith. We human beings are complex composites: feelings, thoughts, images, bones and muscles. As we experience life the whole person comes into contact with the larger world. Since maturity is a long time in coming and conversion is a lifelong process, we are often interiorly divided by events that we label as crises and tragedies. Lewis, just like the rest of us, struggled violently when death touched his life. Enter into the confusion and anxiety of this reflection:

> Feelings, and feelings, and feelings. Let me try thinking instead. From the rational point of view, what new factor has H's death introduced into the problem of the universe? What grounds has it given me for doubting all that I believe? I knew already that these things, and worse, happened daily. I would have said that I had taken them into account. I had been warned—I had warned myself—not to reckon on worldly happiness. We were even promised sufferings. They were part of the programme. We were even told "Blessed are they that mourn" and I accepted it. I've got nothing that I hadn't bargained for. Of course it is different when the thing happens to oneself, not to others, and in reality, not in imagination. Yes, but should it, for a sane man, make quite such a difference as this? No. And it wouldn't for a man whose faith had been real faith and whose concern for other people's sorrows had been real concern. The case is too plain. If my house has collapsed at one blow, that is because it was a house of cards. The faith which "took the set things into account" was not faith but imagination. The taking them into account was not real sympathy. If I had really cared, as I thought I did,

about the sorrows of the world, I should not have
been so over-whelmed when my own sorrow came.
It has been an imaginary faith playing with
innocuous counters labeled "Illness", "Pain",
"Death" and "Loneliness". I thought I trusted the
rope until it mattered to me whether it would bear
me. Now it matters, and I find I didn't.[1]

Several times C. S. Lewis describes his faith as something
without foundation or substance, a mere "house of
cards." For those of us who, as youngsters, learn the art of
constructing card houses, we know well that the slightest
miscue or any sudden draft will bring the paper house
down in utter ruin. Lewis was a theologian. He had the
erudition and language system to speak about the
mysteries of faith in a coherent and consistent manner.
His house was firmly rational and defensible. But faith is
more a matter of experience than it is of logical content.
When his wife Joy died, Lewis came to the painful
realization that his faith was extremely fragile.

Consider: *What images do you have of your faith life?*

Faith is essentially a matter of trust. The image of a rope
conveys, by way of analogy, the issue of reliance we place
on some material object. Are we or are we not willing to
trust the strands of these fibers? As one climbs the
mountains we rely on the slender rope that holds us in
place above canyon floors. If the rope breaks we plummet
to our death; if the rope holds, we climb in safety.

Consider: *How many strands are there in your "faith rope"?*

Imagination, that marvelous and creative faculty, is not
faith. Too easily we imagine what God is like, who we are,
what life and death are all about. Too often reality is so
terribly different. The gospel refuses to indulge

romanticism. The Christian journey is one that assures us of suffering as well as of eternal joys, deep sorrow as well as everlasting life. A mature faith does not stop at the border of the senses, intelligence or memory. Rather, it offers a radical yes to whatever is God's will.

Consider: *How do faith and imagination differ?*

Now we will consider death as a phase in life's journey. In the movie *Shadowlands*, a film narrating the love relationship between C. S. Lewis and Joy Davidman Gresham, we witness how these two struggling pilgrims faced the awesome mystery of death, a death which was cruel in its execution and trying to their world. After a strange courtship involving the tensions of her divorce, church regulations and considerable peer pressure, Lewis and Gresham experienced deep married love. It was to be short-termed. A few months after their marriage, Joy was diagnosed with breast cancer and later with bone cancer. With sensitivity and compassion the movie captures well the effort these two Christians made in attempting to integrate death into the full map of life. Lewis writes:

> And then one or the other dies. And we think of this as love cut short; like a dance stopped in mid-career or a flower with its head unluckily snapped off— something truncated and therefore, lacking its due shape. I wonder. If, as I can't help suspecting, the dead also feel the pains of separation (and this may be one of their purgatorial sufferings), then for both lovers, and for all pairs of lovers without exception, bereavement is a universal and integral part of our experience of love. It follows marriage as normally as marriage follows courtship or as autumn follows summer. It is not a truncation of the process but one of its phases; not the interruption of the dance, but the next figure. We are "taken out of ourselves" by

the loved one while she is here. Then comes the
tragic figure of the dance in which we must learn to
be still taken out of ourselves though the bodily
presence is withdrawn, to love the very Her, and not
fall back to loving our past, or our memory, or our
sorrow, or our relief from sorrow, or our own love.[2]

Emily Dickinson wrote of a happy flower that was
suddenly beheaded by an unexpected frost. This in itself
was sad news but sadder still was the reflection that God
apparently approved of the flower's demise and the sun
was indifferent as the "blond assassin" (the frost) did its
cruel deed. When death comes, not to a flower, but to a
parent, a wife, a child, then we are in for a severe testing.

Consider: *What was the most painful bereavement of your
life? What meaning have you discovered in it since it
happened?*

As C. S. Lewis thought out his grief in writing, he came to
the realization that bereavement is an essential component
of life and love. It is a natural phase that, however painful,
must be integrated into our understanding of the mystery
of life. Since we rebel at loss and separation, it is not
surprising that we attempt to deny this bereavement
phase of life. We, on the natural level, shy away from
sacrifice which explains why voluntary bereavement
rarely occurs.

Consider: *How can bereavement become life-giving and not
destructive?*

What does bereavement do? It can destroy us, turning us
down the lane of self-pity. Or it can "take us out of
ourselves," proving a strange sort of ecstasy that refuses to
live on memories which are often distorted and thus
unreal. Bereavement is a chapter in life's book, a chapter

as significant and important as any other. Death appears as an interruption if not a termination of life's dance. It is difficult to conceive of bereavement as a life-giving process. A deep faith is necessary if our autobiographies are to be complete, a faith that sees through death and loss into the light of the resurrection.

Consider: *How can bereavement become ecstasy? Where are you in the process of integrating bereavement into your life? Has it become life-giving, a kind of ecstasy in Lewis's terms?*

The doctrine of the communion of saints provides a firm hope. Those who have preceded us in death have entered into the presence of God and God's holy people. Like the risen Christ they intercede for us, concerned with our well-being. From their place in heaven, they see us still and continue to share their love.

> It is often thought that the dead see us. And we assume, whether reasonably or not, that if they see us at all they see us more clearly than before. Does H. now see exactly how much froth or tinsel there was in what she called, and I call, my love? So be it. We didn't idealize each other. We tried to keep no secrets. You knew most of the rotten places in me already. If you now see anything worse, I can take it. So can you. Rebuke, explain, mock, forgive. For this is one of the miracles of love; it gives—to both, but perhaps especially to the woman—a power of seeing through its own enchantments and yet not being disenchanted.
>
> To see, in some measure, like God. His love and His knowledge are not distinct from one another, nor from Him. We could almost say He sees because He loves, and therefore loves although He sees.[3]

Do the dead see us? Is the Catholic doctrine of the communion of saints a basic faith fact? Our relationship with them is living and active. And there is to be no nonsense here, no romanticism. The saints see through our defense mechanisms, our tinsel facades, our guilt activism. There is no room for idolization. Truth will win out and, of course, it will set us free.

Consider: *Of those who have preceded you in death, whose gaze do you feel most often?*

C. S. Lewis speaks of the miracles of love. One of these happens by way of a type of seeing that penetrates the illusions of fascination while not yielding to a debilitating pessimism. Thus the miracle: to see all, the healthy as well as the rotten places, and still not be disenchanted. Much grace is needed here. Only the power of the Holy Spirit can empower us to see "the dearest freshness deep down things."

Consider: *What has been your experience of the miracles of love?*

For Reflection

When God looks, God loves, so says the great contemplative, Saint John of the Cross. The profound mystery is that we cannot separate God's knowing from divine loving. In Jesus this mystery became incarnate. Seeing is enfleshed in doing, in a perfect obedience. Nothing is of greater urgency than to develop "soft eyes," eyes that are loving despite the presence of so much disease, darkness and evil. The "dead" see us because they are alive in love, experiencing the mystery of the Resurrection and the glory of God. How can we begin to see like God does?

Closing Prayer

"Down, down, down into the darkness of the grave
Gently they go, the beautiful, the tender, the kind;
Quietly they go, the intelligent, the witty, the brave.
I know. But I do not approve. And I am not resigned."

—Edna St. Vincent Millay,
"Dirge Without Music"

God of the living and the dead,
in the darkness of faith we believe in the
    Resurrection.
Yet we find it so hard to yield to death,
the dawn that brings the fullness of day.
Are we in the shadowlands?
Is death the passage into full life and light?
Send your Spirit of faith upon us
and may the risen Lord assure us of his peace.
We beg this through that same Savior.

Notes

[1] C. S. Lewis, *A Grief Observed* (New York: The Seabury Press, 1961), p. 31.
[2] *A Grief Observed*, p. 41.
[3] *A Grief Observed*, pp. 56-57.

Going Forth to Live the Theme

"Let's stay in touch": an expression indicating that people are interested in sustaining and deepening a relationship. We can pursue this in various ways—writing letters, making phone calls, sending e-mail, scheduling lunch or vacation, praying for one another.

But how do we further our acquaintance with those who have died, those who have gone to that far distant country? More precisely, how do we further our acquaintance with C. S. Lewis? I offer three suggestions.

First, memorize a poem by Lewis. Many people do not realize that Lewis was a poet. My suggestion that you memorize a poem comes from the radical conviction that when we truly appropriate and internalize the thoughts, feelings and words of another, especially in poetic form, we achieve an understanding and bonding that is at once deep and intimate. A poem is an expression of the poet's soul. To welcome it into our own soul, with courtesy and reverence, is a profound encounter.

On Being Human

Angelic minds, they say, by simple intelligence
Behold the Forms of nature. They discern
Unerringly the Archtypes, all the verities
Which mortals lack or indirectly learn.
Transparent in primordial truth, unvarying,
Pure Earthness and right Stonehood from their clear,
High eminence are seen; unveiled, the seminal
    Huge Principles appear.

The Tree-ness of the tree they know—the meaning of
Arboreal life, how from earth's salty lap
The solar beam uplifts it, all the holiness
Enacted by leaves' fall and rising sap;
But never an angel knows the knife-edged severance
Of sun from shadow where the trees begin,
The blessed cool at every pore caressing us
    An angel has no skin.

They see the Form of Air; but mortals breathing it
Drink the whole summer down into the breast.
The lavish pinks, the field new-mown, the ravishing
Sea-smells, the wood-fire smoke that whispers Rest.
The tremor on the rippled pool of memory
That from each smell in widening circles goes,
The pleasure and the pang—can angels measure it?
    An angel has no nose.

The nourishing of life, and how it flourishes
On death, and why, they utterly know; but not
The hill-born, earthy spring, the dark cold bilberries
The ripe peach from the southern wall still hot,
Full-bellied tankards foamy-topped, the delicate
Half-lyric lamb, a new loaf's billowy curves,
Nor porridge, nor the tingling taste of oranges—
    An angel has no nerves.

Far richer they! I know the senses' witchery
Guards us, like air, from heavens too big to see;
Imminent death to man that bard's sublimity
And dazzling edge of beauty unsheathed would be.
Yet here, within this tiny, charm'd interior,
This parlour of the brain, their Maker shares
With living men some secrets in a privacy
    Forever ours, not theirs.[1]

If that verse is a little too long, here is a shorter one no
less powerful:

After Prayers, Lie Cold

Arise my body, my small body, we have striven
Enough, and He is merciful; we are forgiven.
Arise small body, puppet-like and pale, and go,
White as the bed-clothes into bed, and cold as snow,
Undress with small, cold fingers and put out the light,
And be alone, hush'd mortal, in the sacred night,
—A meadow whipt flat with the rain, a cup
Emptied and clean, a garment washed and folded up,
Faded in colour, thinned almost to raggedness
By dirt and by the washing of that dirtiness.
Be not too quickly warm again. Lie cold; consent
To weariness' and pardon's watery element.
Drink up the bitter water, breathe the chilly death;
Soon enough comes the riot of our blood and breath.[2]

Furthering our acquaintance through this suggestion is
not easy. It demands time, effort and concentration. The
end product of a deeper friendship is worth the
commitment.

A second suggestion: Read the letters of C. S. Lewis.
Unlike Lewis's theological essays, literary monographs,
fiction and poetry, his letters offer a personal and unique
revelation of a man truly concerned about others,
perceptive in his understanding of the human condition,
wise in sharing insight and friendly advice. Lewis is a
skilled letter-writer.

Here are a few of my favorite excerpts:

I also have become much acquainted with grief now
through the death of my great friend Charles
Williams, my friend of friends, the comforter of all
our little set, the most angelic man. The odd thing is

that his death has made my faith stronger than it was
a week ago. And I find that all that talk about
"feeling that he is closer to us than before" isn't just
talk. It's just what it does feel like—I can't put it into
words. One seems at moments to be living in a new
world. Lots, lots of pain, but not a particle of
depression or resentment.[3]

You needn't worry about not feeling brave. Our Lord
didn't—see the scene in Gethsemane. How thankful I
am that when God became man He did not choose to
become a man of iron nerves; that would not have
helped weaklings like you and me nearly so much.[4]

The process of living seems to consist in coming to
realize truths so ancient and simple that, if stated,
they would sound like barren platitudes. They
cannot sound otherwise to those who have not had
the relevant experience: that is why there is no real
teaching of such truths possible and every generation
starts from scratch.[5]

A third and final suggestion. Read one of the two
following biographies:

William Griffin's *Clive Staples Lewis: A Dramatic Life* (San
Francisco: Harper & Row, Publishers, 1986), 507
pages.

A. N. Wilson's *C. S. Lewis: A Biography* (New York: W. W.
Norton & Company, 1990), 334 pages.

A line attributed to Saint Thomas Aquinas brings this
volume to a close: "No possession is joyous without a
companion." C. S. Lewis is a mighty good companion,
bringing to us much joy.

Notes

[1] *C. S. Lewis: Poems*, edited by Walter Hooper (San Diego: Harcourt Brace Jovanovich, 1964), pp. 34-35.

[2] *Poems*, p. 130.

[3] *Letters of C. S. Lewis*, ed. by W. H. Lewis (New York: Harcourt Brace Jovanovich, 1966), p. 206.

[4] *Letters*, p. 250.

[5] *Letters*, p. 166.

Deepening Your Acquaintance

Books

Lewis, C. S. *The Abolition of Man*. New York: Macmillan, 1947.

_____. *The Four Loves*. New York: Harcourt Brace Jovanovich, 1960.

_____. *Grief Observed*. New York: Bantam, 1976.

_____. *Mere Christianity*. New York: Macmillan, 1970.

_____. *The Screwtape Letters*. New York: Macmillan, 1982.

_____. *Surprised by Joy: The Shape of My Early Life*. New York: Harcourt Brace Jovanovich, 1955.

Videos

Both of the following film versions of *Shadowlands* are fictionalized accounts of the relationship between C. S. Lewis and Joy Davidman Gresham. They are appealing additions to, rather than substitutes for, Lewis's own books.

Shadowlands (original TV drama). Coproduced by the BBC and Gateway Films. Available from Gateway Films/Vision Video.

Shadowlands (a Richard Attenborough film). Also available from Gateway Films/Vision Video.